# SECRE
## OF THE
# AUTISTIC
# MILLIONAIRE

*Everything I know about Autism, ASD, and Asperger's that I wish I'd known back then...*

David William Plummer

**Copyright © 2021-2023 by David William Plummer**

All rights reserved worldwide. No part of this book may be reproduced or transmitted in any form or by any means, electronic or mechanical, including photocopying, recording, or by an information storage and retrieval system - except by a reviewer who may quote brief passages in a review - without permission in writing from the publisher.

**Published by Plummer's Software LLC, Redmond WA, 98074**

Set in Bookman Old Style and Century Gothic

Document Version V12-23.02.09

| | | |
|---|---|---|
| ISBN | 9798498617725 | Paperback |
| | 9798754616820 | Hardcover |
| ASIN | B09KGF6685 | eBook |

# Advanced Praise for Secrets of the Autistic Millionaire

*"Dave gives both parents and teachers lots of helpful insights on how he progressed from being an autistic child to a successful computer programmer at Microsoft."*

-Temple Grandin, Ph.D.

# Acknowledgements

My sincere thanks to everyone who reviewed advance copies of this book, particularly the early drafts.  So many people contributed their thoughts and corrections that any attempt to enumerate them all now would be so unacceptably incomplete that I must simply issue a big group thank-you to everyone involved!  But a few folks, ranging from old friends like Glen Hodges to old coworkers like Brian Aust to new acquaintances like Eric Lawrence, gave so extensively of their time and effort that I must specifically call them out.  I truly appreciate the assistance and encouragement, without which I would never have finished this work.  Without Ben Slivka's ignition, it would never have even begun.

I'd like to thank Craig Pyette for his early review and encouragement, without which I likely would not have believed in my own ability enough to continue the project in earnest.  I would also like to thank Temple Grandin, Ph.D., for her draft review, feedback, encouragement, and for her permission to use materials from her TED Talk.

I think many people with Autism Spectrum Disorder get nervous about trying new things, and I do write a bit like a big skittish deer; at first, a chapter here and there to see what my wife thinks. If she likes it, then other neurotypical people will probably like it too, and I take another step.  And so it has been with almost *everything* I've done for 30 years.  Thank you, Nikki, for always being there to coax me out of the woods, and for occasionally chasing me down when I got spooked.

At some point the perfect becomes the enemy of the good and I had to "ship it", meaning there are inevitably still bugs worth fixing in here.

If you spot ANY mistakes, errors, or omissions, please contact the publisher **immediately** at

> highpriority@theautisticmillionaire.com

# CONTENTS

Dedication ................................................................... ix

About this Book and its Title ................................... ix

*Introduction: Welcome to Autism* ........................... 1

    Burgers with Bill Gates ............................................. 1

    Wait, I've Got What? ................................................. 4

    What's Inside This Book ........................................... 9

*A History of the Autistic Millionaire* ..................... 13

    Before the Beginning ............................................. 13

    From 7-Eleven to Microsoft .................................. 25

    Coming to America ................................................. 32

*Understanding Autism* .............................................. 75

    Neurodiversity versus Disorder ........................... 76

    Person with Autism vs Autistic Person .............. 77

    Autism Severity ....................................................... 80

    A Personal Tour of Autism Symptoms ............... 83

*Living with Autism* .................................................. 119

    Emotions ................................................................. 119

    Empathy .................................................................. 125

    Mindblindness ....................................................... 133

    Monofocus, Hyperfocus and Bracketing ......... 138

- Arguing with Autism .................................................................. 141
- Bullying and Teasing ................................................................. 148
- Coordination and Movement .................................................. 153
- Stimming .................................................................................... 159
- Resistance to Change ............................................................... 162

## *Secrets of the Autistic Millionaire* .................................................. *166*

- Autism and Autism on the Job ................................................ 167
- Parenting with Autism ............................................................. 178
- Love and Relationships with Autism ..................................... 192
- Masking ...................................................................................... 216
- Low Frustration Tolerance ...................................................... 222
- Accommodations ..................................................................... 226
- Meltdowns ................................................................................. 234
- Anger ......................................................................................... 245
- Making Friends with Autism .................................................. 251
- A Reason for Being .................................................................. 265

## *Afterword* ................................................................................ *272*

- The Ten-Second Autism Test ................................................. 272
- Sources ...................................................................................... 275
- About the Author ..................................................................... 276

## Dedication

This book is dedicated to my four children, each of whom has inherited both gift and burden in their own unique amount and proportion by having selected me to be their biological father. It is said that the apple does not fall far from the tree; may a better understanding of the tree provide you with greater insight into the apple.

## About this Book and its Title

This book is intended both for individuals who are on the autism spectrum (or who suspect that they may be), and for those who live, work, love, and play with them. It is a book about living a happy, successful, productive, and fulfilling life with autism, and it includes everything that I wish I had known about autism far earlier in my life. While the title may understandably lead one to believe that this is a book about financial success, money is only one metric by which success can be measured. How *you* define success is largely a personal decision; this book is about enabling that success regardless of how you measure it.

# Introduction: Welcome to Autism

## Burgers with Bill Gates

The first time I met Bill was almost thirty years ago in his backyard. A pair of burly security guards dressed in too-tight purple Microsoft polo shirts politely escorted me through his home on the West Side of Lake Washington. It was a mansion to my mid-western eyes, though only a fraction the size of the more famous home he would later build sprawling across the hillsides of the lake's eastern shore. Windows 95 was still in the future, and I was at Microsoft working on the older operating system known as MS-DOS. I was just a temporary intern -- not even a full-time "blue badge" employee yet -- but back in those days, Microsoft was small enough to allow Bill to invite the top college prospects over for a backyard BBQ.

Out on the lawn with a microbrew in hand, we all clustered around him, hoping to catch his interest in conversation. Each of us had no doubt prepared something clever to say, just in case the opportunity presented itself: perhaps an insight about, or criticism of, a Microsoft product so perceptive or biting that he'd recognize our innate genius amongst the crowd and pluck us, like a gem, from the front lines. That was the daydream. The starker reality was that after our burger and beer we'd be hurried out the front door and back to headquarters in

Redmond to work another of our 16-hour days, competing directly against one another for the top spots. Everyone came from the best schools: MIT and Princeton in the United States, Waterloo in Canada. With over 100,000 job applications coming into Microsoft every year at the time, just *being* one of those 30 was an incredibly big deal -- especially if you were from the University of Regina like I was.

That's in Saskatchewan if that helps any, but either way, I was only really at Microsoft by virtue of having put myself through college on the proceeds from writing software for a competing computer platform. My program, HyperCache, had already sold a few thousand copies before it popped up on Microsoft's radar. My task now was to write something like it for their MS-DOS, releasing it for a hundred million PCs instead of just a few thousand. If that went well, there was a good chance of a full-time spot upon graduation – complete with their famously lucrative Microsoft stock options. Failing that, I could always go back to my old job at 7-Eleven (and so you can imagine why I wanted to make a good first impression).

We gathered in concentric circles around Bill as the setting sun glistened off the lake behind us. Few dared probe toward the center, where Bill himself stood alone, but I had an advantage with Ben, my manager. He knew Bill and seemed completely unfazed by fame or fortune. Ben pulled me straight through the gauntlet of would-be nerds and presented me directly to Bill as if I were a prized protégé.

He told him: "This is Dave, our intern from Canada. In the space of four months…" his voice trailed off to list the very real technical accomplishments that I had worked so hard to complete that summer. I listened in earnestness at first, but soon became highly distracted with one very real problem: it hadn't *technically* been four months as Ben had said. It had only taken three months -- not four.

It was a small thing, but an important detail. I was sure they'd want to know. I cleared my throat, spoke up, and interrupted them with the correction:

"Three months."

Surprised, they both stopped, turned, and looked at me. My heart sank. Once again -- as always -- I had spoken out of turn, somehow saying just the wrong thing at precisely the wrong time. That much was obvious, and that was three decades ago.

And yet I just found out *last week* that I have autism! (I'm writing this part raw, in the aftermath of that diagnosis, to capture my early thoughts about it.)

Ben and I had both long since moved on from Microsoft, and I had not seen him in several years. At some point along the way he had been surprised by a diagnosis of autism spectrum disorder for his own adult daughter, and apparently, after better understanding the symptoms and seeing them in the context of his own family, one of his early thoughts was "Dave should get himself tested." Soon after, he took me for lunch and told me about his daughter's diagnosis, and without really being specific at all as to why, he encouraged me to investigate being tested for autism myself.

I wasn't really bothered by the idea, but I was a bit confused as to what would lead him to think so. I went home and took the

Autism Spectrum Quotient test online and, of a possible fifty points, I scored forty. Clearly, I thought, I must be answering the questions with personal bias, so I had my wife of twenty-five years sit down and make sure I was being accurate and honest. I retook the test with her to be sure that I did not exaggerate. My score went up: forty-two.

For years I had joked that "I'm not on the spectrum, but you can *see* it from here." I later upgraded that to "I might be on the spectrum, but I'm on the non-visible portion." Still, I didn't really consider it possible. I'm empathetic, sensitive, emotional, and funny -- all things that I thought would preclude me from being anywhere on the autism spectrum.

## Wait, I've Got What?

> *I used to be "gifted," but now I had a "diagnosis"...*
>
> *...and it had a "better" and a "worse."*

I booked the necessary appointments and over the course of a few weeks completed all the testing. I would have done better on the SAT and math sections with a little advanced practice but going in cold as an adult was also interesting in its own right. It sure had been a long time since I'd done much long division! Preparing the full report took a few weeks, and my wife accompanied me to receive the results.

The good news? Apparently, I'm reasonably clever. As in "three standard deviations" smart. On some portions of the cognitive testing, I even achieved perfection -- something they'd apparently never seen before. But I was also *slow*. I got the right answer but took my own sweet time to get it. Each test runs to completion without you knowing the time limit, but they watch and record where you were at when the set time limit expired. I scored very highly on the SAT but *only* if time wasn't considered: had I been cut off at the official time limit, I would have only scored 1,150, a fairly average score. The reason? Apparently, I have serious Attention Deficit Disorder. Oh, and as noted: it also turns out that I have autism.

More accurately, I was officially diagnosed with autism spectrum disorder. As the doctor, my wife, and I flipped through the pages of the report in unison, terms like "significant social dysfunction" stared back at me. When we finally got to the autism-specific behaviors section, my wife was pleased to note: "Well, at least the numbers are good here, far above average!" -- but then the doctor corrected her:

"No, no... higher is *worse*."

I used to be "gifted," but now I had a "diagnosis." And it had a "better" and a "worse." That's about all I felt in those initial minutes.

Not everyone appreciates popular media portrayals of autism, but we'll leave that aside, for now, to make use of two such examples as handy measuring devices: if I were forced to use a pop reference as perhaps the least accurate but most communicative way to express the amount of autism that I am affected by, I would say I have 80% as much as Sheldon Cooper on *The Big Bang Theory*. At current exchange rates, I'd estimate that makes me about 25% as autistic as the title character in the movie *Rain Man*. As you can guess these are *not* professional metrics, they're numbers pulled from the air by a layman*.

From the actual test report, I can see that I'm more autistic than roughly 98.5% of the general population. While that might sound quite "autistic", I'm still fairly "high functioning." I don't use those terms a lot, however. I'm also highly *impacted* in many ways -- which is what makes my "balance" point interesting, I believe. In short, I'm far enough into it to deeply understand the autism thought process that is normally inaccessible to neurotypical people, yet still conversant enough to explain back to everyone what they are missing -- and even how this condition can be of use in their own lives at times. Hopefully, I can explain it to you!

Unfortunately, as with many people on the spectrum, my brain is "complicated" in other ways as well. As I noted earlier, I have significant attention deficit disorder (ADD) (my mother says she would add hyperactivity to the list, but I was never tested as a youth). I also, to my great regret, smoked cigarettes for thirty years, and I believe it was that stimulant that allowed me to manage my dopamine and stay focused for most of my adult

---

* When I told my closest and most curmudgeonly 70-year-old combat-veteran mechanic friend that testing had revealed me to be "a little autistic," his flat reply was: "Just a little, huh?" -- So apparently not everyone was surprised. -- We will discuss the possibility of being "a little autistic" in later chapters.

life. This probably explains why the ADD only really came to light when I quit smoking (or while sitting without them for long exams, depositions, etc.). On top of this, I've also suffered from anxiety, which has been known to lead to bouts of depression if not well managed.

Or could it be that these are just aspects of my autism, mischaracterized as unrelated anxiety and mood disorders for decades? These were among the questions I would attempt to answer for myself.

Learning these things about myself didn't happen all at once. In fact, it has been a process of discovery over the course of more than 25 years, treating problems and issues whenever and wherever they arose without systematically looking for a deeper connection between them. That I did not *eventually* diagnose my own autism surprises me. I don't feel bad for missing it, however, given that for decades more qualified educators and professionals also overlooked the same symptoms. To be honest, however, I cannot blame them either: over the years I've become a master at "masking," or the art of acting "normal", which makes a diagnosis without specific testing even more difficult. Girls are reportedly even better at such masking, going undiagnosed even more often as a result.

The good news is that this odd mix of brain disorder and ability has not caused my life to descend entirely into chaos: in fact, quite the contrary. Although it has been a wild ride at times for both myself and those around me, this exotic brain of mine has served me incredibly well! If you will briefly indulge some self-congratulatory details: I graduated at the top of my university with an engineering degree (though years late in starting it because I had dropped out of high school); I have made multiple fortunes many different ways; I have invented, designed, and engineered products used daily by billions of humans around the globe; been issued half a dozen patents; started my own company in my den that went on to achieve over one-hundred-million dollars in sales; married my beautiful soulmate; raised four happy and successful children... and much more. And yet, for all this self-indulgent list of success, privilege, and grace, I still struggle with simple things like eye contact... and conversation flow... and relationships, and anger, and anxiety, and meltdowns, and a dozen other things we shall soon turn to look at.

It is only now, in retrospect, that I can look back and see specifically where certain aspects of autism impacted my life, for better and for worse, and it is here that I tell those stories. If I am successful, it will be because I not only explain and entertain, but I will have done so in a way that empowers you to apply some of those lessons learned to your own life -- whether you are personally affected by autism or not. Because to be clear, life with *some* autism can be spectacular!

# What's Inside This Book

Within these pages, I have four related goals. The first is to give you a better understanding of high-functioning individuals with autism -- the real Sheldon Coopers* of the world if you

*"I'm convinced that about half of what separates successful entrepreneurs from the non-successful ones is pure perseverance."*

*Steve Jobs*

will. I want you to understand what makes us tick, what we think, why we think it, how we act upon it, and why we do it that way. From there the book will take an in-depth look at some important autism topics, often from multiple perspectives. For example, the chapter on employment considers both what it means to be managed by an autistic manager as well as what it takes to manage an autistic employee. The vantage point will continue to shift as we tackle topics such as parenting and marriage. The second goal is to

---

* A fictional character from the television show "The Big Bang Theory" that was widely assumed to be on the autism spectrum.

help you understand specifically what makes some of those with autism so relentless in their pursuit of success. After identifying and discussing those traits and attributes, my goal is to help those with similar traits capitalize on them. Perhaps if a neurotypical person reading this can understand the characteristics, routines, and habits of certain individuals with autism, they too will be able to increase their odds of success through learning new approaches for their own lives.

There is no easy way to know if public figures such as Bill Gates, Jeff Bezos, and Mark Zuckerberg are on the autism spectrum. If they are, none have publicly shared that information, and unless and until they do, it's a private health matter that I won't speculate on. We can, however, observe and identify certain traits and characteristics that they exhibit in common with people on the spectrum and note how they may have served to make those individuals so driven to succeed in their own endeavors, *regardless* of whether they experience the disorder or not. Which is almost the point: irrespective of who is officially diagnosed with what condition, if something worked for me, and it worked for them, it *might* work for you!

A third goal is to entertain you along the way, as it has been *quite* an interesting journey: not just for me, but for the loved ones around me, who must have sometimes felt as untethered as I did.

**The tales of how autism has impacted my life and career are not here merely for the vicarious enjoyment of others. I truly believe that for someone with the disorder, and for those close to that person, both knowing how I persevered and**

**seeing where I stumbled and failed can be useful and instructive.**

The fourth and final goal is to help assure loved ones, especially any parents of children newly diagnosed with autism (at least those at a level of severity like my own). Having a diagnosis in hand can make things much easier to manage. In truth, this perceived responsibility I feel toward parents of such children remains my primary motivation in "coming out" about my autism. If I had known in my youth what I know now, my life would have been even better... or at least a much easier journey. Knowing that in just a few chapters I could tell you things that took me (and my family) a lifetime to learn by trial and error was a driving factor in me completing this book. In this way, I hope to possibly save you a great deal of angst and misery!

If you come along on this journey you'll watch as I go from being a bullied youth to winding up a high school dropout, then turn my life around sharply enough to return to school and ultimately secure distinguished research grants and scholarships. Next, we'll leave the small farming city in Saskatchewan for Microsoft at the height of the 90s tech boom as I get married, graduate, and emigrate all in one crazy weekend. Follow as I build a company -- starting in my den -- whose sales explode geometrically causing me to sell it for cash to a NASDAQ company. Right at the peak, I will be sued by the government, federally compliance-audited, *and* state tax-audited all at once during the sale, potentially scuttling the entire deal and prompting an autistic meltdown right in the offices of the attorney general!

Moving on from my personal experience with autism we will look at selected topics related to the disorder. Because autism is probably still new for most of us, we can follow the standard model of instruction: "Here's what I tried, and here's what worked and what did not, and why I think that is." We will follow that approach for important topics related to autism, such as Empathy, Emotions, Masking, Mindblindness, Marriage, Parenting, Employment, and many more. By the end of this book, you will know a great deal more about what it's like to live with autism, and for those that were already keenly aware, you will learn a few secrets for staying sane and being successful: the things that I have discovered along the way.

Finally, we shall turn to some more speculative topics. As we unwind the complex attributes, characteristics, methods, and mannerisms of those with autism I believe there is much to be learned by neurotypical people as well. What caused the obsessive drive towards success in some people with autism? And if this is identifiable, can it be emulated? Are medical students cramming for board exams really "faking autism" selectively for brief periods? Can someone really be a "little bit autistic"? Should people with autism "fake it" to make friends, and where should the limits of such masking end? Are some movies and television shows with autistic characters as exploitive as some would assert? We will consider all these issues and more.

# A History of the Autistic Millionaire

## Before the Beginning

### An Initial Encounter with Autism

My first real education on autism came years ago, as it did for many people, in the form of Dustin Hoffman's portrayal of the eponymous lead character in the movie *Rain Man*. Hoffman's *Rain Man*, based in part upon the real-life story of Kim Peek, was someone then known as an "autistic savant" with many exceptional abilities. Peek was said to have read entire books by scanning the left page with his left eye while scanning the other with his right. He was also believed to have near-perfect retention of some twelve thousand different books; this was but one of his many amazing intellectual abilities.

At the same time, however, *Rain Man* suffered from profound social, interpersonal, and various cognitive deficits, forcing him to live in an institution with full-time care. For all his massive intellectual horsepower in certain areas, he was unlikely to have been able to perform his own grocery shopping. Such is but one conundrum of autism: quite often a high price is demanded without commensurate compensation in the form of apparent gifts.

Not every person with significant autism is also a savant. Conversely, not every brilliant yet introverted scientist should be presumed to have autism. I had no idea that I had it: not even the slightest inkling. I knew I was different. I knew I was smarter than average, introverted, passionate about technology, and that I had some behaviors that (on the surface) were also common in people that had autism. Even so, the idea that I personally could have autism was completely alien and *never* occurred to me until perhaps my mid-forties. Even then, I just assumed that I had a few symptoms in concordance with autism, not that I actually *had* the disorder. Right up until the test results came back, I was almost entirely oblivious to my own condition.

Once I knew authoritatively that I was indeed on the spectrum, two important things happened. First, my understanding of autism expanded, leading me to appreciate just how wide the autism spectrum is. There are people with autism, like our *Rain Man*, who are much more profoundly impacted by its symptoms--and there are many who are far less affected than I. The range of neurodiversity even within the autism spectrum is impressive.

Second, as with any condition one finds themselves troubled by, I became curious: how did I come to have autism? There are no environmental triggers or causes known. I had been vaccinated as a child but the link that had once been fraudulently asserted between vaccines and autism had long ago been so fully discredited that I gave it no serious consideration. That really left only one: genetics. While autism does indeed seem to have its roots in our genes, the heritability of autism is complex, and no one knows specifically which genes contribute to the condition. It's also possible that environmental factors work in concert with genetics and epigenetics to form a cause. Some have speculated that autism is perhaps an over-representation of "technical" genes; these genes are likely the very same ones that led to the discovery of stone tools, fire, and other early technologies. As the author Temple Grandin has written, without those genes the human race might still be socializing around campfires!

## Where Did my Autism Come From?

Neither my parents nor my grandparents, nor any of their siblings, had autism, and I'm not aware of any autism in my distant family history. To say that my family tree is narrow would be an understatement--in fact, both of my parents grew up without siblings, as only children. I'm not sure what to make of the fact that the evolutionary tree narrowed to a single branch when I was born, but it almost didn't make it *that* far: my father was only an hour old when his heart stopped for the first time.

*My father and grandparents before the fateful ride.*

Dad was delivered by a small-town doctor in a little wood-frame house during the opening days of World War II in Rocanville, Saskatchewan, in 1940. After being born he fought for about an hour, struggling before he simply ran out of energy and his little heart stopped beating. By some stroke of fate, the country doctor on hand had recently returned from a medical conference in America, where he'd attended a seminar on the use of cardiac adrenaline; curiosity and necessity met, and the drug was injected deep into my father's heart muscle. Within a few moments, first came a twitch, and then a cry: it was enough to revive him and save my father's life even before it had truly begun.

Not long after it had begun, however, that young life nearly came crashing to an early end. When he was a small child, my dad was riding in the back seat of an old Ford that featured rear "suicide doors," those which open outward on rear hinges. The name hails from the unfortunate reality of what happens if a rear door is opened while driving down the highway, or, indeed, if perhaps a young child plays with the interior handle at the wrong moment -- the door flies open, becoming an instant air brake, violently sucking the contents of the back seat -- my young father included -- haphazardly onto the highway at 45 miles per hour. His head smacked the roadway, knocking him instantly and solidly unconscious. Yet somehow, he was still alive.

Hours from any form of emergency medical care, his parents did what they could, which is to say, very little: they tended to his road rash and other injuries until he finally awoke some 45 minutes later. Dad's only memory from the incident was of a man in white watching over him as he slept.

Throughout his life, my father had cerebral palsy (CP) affecting primarily the right side of his body. Conventional family wisdom attributes this to the traumatic brain injury suffered when he fell out of that car, but most medical experts I've spoken to point to the oxygen deprivation likely to have accompanied the circumstances of his birth as the most probable cause. Apparently, the symptoms of this type of brain injury can take some time to manifest. In the end, it's immaterial whether it started at birth or at a few years of age, but the fact that my Dad grew up as a teenager in the 1950s labeled by some as a "cripple" was formative upon his personality, both for better and for worse. As an example, when his ability to even play a musical instrument was doubted, he opted for the saxophone on the grounds that it seemed the most challenging. Learning to master its complicated fingering could not have been easy given his tremors, but he persevered and later played professionally as a young man.

My father was brilliant, stubborn, and relentless in ways that could be consistent with being on the spectrum but without the social deficits: he owned and operated our family hardware store for decades, he was great with people across all walks of life in a way that implied a natural ability to understand and connect with them; it was not merely a masking performance.

As an interesting aside* my dad was right-handed, meaning that his dominant control side was also the side most affected

---

* People with autism seem to love to take you on these little related-but-trivial "interesting aside" adventures where they relate tangential information that feels fascinating to them, and I'm no exception. I will try to limit them to footnotes, because unlike a friend with autism, footnotes can wait until later!

by his cerebral palsy. Because of this, from an early age, he was forced by the adults around him out of the perceived necessity to learn to write with his left hand. To the end of his days his handwriting, scratched out with his left, looked much the same as my own left-handed handwriting. It never improved throughout his lifetime. Based on his example, at least, you cannot learn to be left-handed no matter *how* long you try.

Fortunately, in contrast, my mother's experiences with emergency medical care have not usually been as the recipient, but rather as the nurse in attendance. After growing up on farms and in a series of small towns in rural Saskatchewan*, she attended nursing school. During that time, she also met my father, and upon graduating Mom worked in some of the most demanding departments possible over her lifetime: the operating room theatre before I was born, and later intensive care and the burns unit.

Medical professionals must manage their empathy, so perhaps having a muted sense of it would not be a great deficit. I'm confident, however, that whatever makes a great nurse -- whatever skill it is that gives someone the ability to be comforting and encouraging while at the same time competently debriding your catastrophic burn injury -- must skip a generation, as my mom absolutely has it, but I do not!

---

* Trivia: Elon Musk's mother was also born in my own hometown of Regina, Saskatchewan, Canada.

## In the Beginning

I may not have known I had autism until later in life, but I always knew that I was "different." From the age of three or four on, all my friends drawn from the local neighborhood were four to six years older than I was. Children with autism often mature more slowly than others, but perhaps having a group of older friends helped me compensate for that somewhat. Regardless, being smart for my age enabled me to at least attempt to hang and talk with the older kids, which was great -- except for the fact they were also by definition much larger than me as well.

Combine being small with the inherent lack of coordination and the dorkiness that is classically exhibited by so many of us on the spectrum, and you have a recipe for a lot of bullying. My own childhood experience was no exception. I still vividly remember my father finally putting an end to it, when I was about age six. He discovered one local bully, a teenager -- literally more than twice my age -- beating me in the alley between the houses. It was not the first time this particular kid had done it. My parents had confronted him directly before and then tried to get his parents involved, but they were of no help, saying meekly that "boys will be boys." Caught red-handed in the midst of one of his more savage attacks, the kid boldly told my father, "There's nothing you can do about it. I'm a minor, so you might as well go on home." My dad, unimpressed with the bully's logic and having already exhausted all reasonable means in the past, first took off his wristwatch for effect. Then, as he grabbed the perpetrator and a crumpled fistful of his sweatshirt in his left hand, he twisted round so only I could see him wink at me to let me in on the fact it was all for show. Then he drew back his right fist. The quaking of his cerebral palsy could make him look and sound a little crazed when he was really angry, and the teen's eyes widened as Dad told him:

"I can take an assault rap at $1,000. The only question is whether *you* can take it at $100 per shot."

Back in the 1970s, he might have been completely serious, at least as far as the bully knew, but I knew perfectly well that we didn't have a thousand dollars to waste. He promptly released my tormenter to run off unscathed, and I never had a problem with that kid again.

Over the years I would grow in stature, reaching 6' 2" by high school, and so my problems with bullies faded as my size caught up with -- and eventually exceeded -- that of the other kids. This is not to say that size is a panacea, as a gentle giant simply makes a bigger soft target for many bullies. The only things most bullies truly respect are defense and consequences, and without one or the other, the bullying will continue.

Eventually, I had to provide my *own* consequences, but not every kid with autism will be able to do that -- bullying of kids on the spectrum is a real problem. We act differently and are often *unable* to defend ourselves due to deficits in coordination as well as the temperament required, making tempting targets for a more cowardly bully. It is up to the parents and the school system to protect such children while they are learning, adapting, and surviving in the school environment. One or two times, my own parents had to become involved both with parents of local bullies and with the school system, and that was back in a time when that type of involvement was uncommon. I'm thankful that they cared enough to do so, even if it was uncomfortable for me at the time. We take a closer look at bullying in a later chapter.

Kids with autism often get obsessive about certain topics, and I was no exception to this: by the third or fourth grade I had learned all I could about NASA and the space program, a new and exciting topic in the days of my youth. I built long tables of every space launch, Russian and American, of every probe and lander, manned or unmanned. I knew them all by heart and my teacher, Mrs. Harvey, asked me to write special reports on the subject that kept me engaged in a way that the standard curriculum simply could not.

Not every teacher was so accommodating. One year, the solution for keeping me engaged was effectively to move me ahead by one grade. Then, to "correct" for this unauthorized advancement when discovered a few years later, I was then forced to repeat sixth grade over. In my mind, this felt the same as being unfairly demoted an entire grade, and that left a bad taste that soured me on school and homework for many years to come. I've always been willing to work exceptionally hard at any chance to move ahead, but deeply resent setbacks not of my own making. I am certainly not one who would enjoy playing a game of random "chutes and ladders" with my own life! I like to make my own luck whenever it's possible.

## OCD—Obsessive Computer Disorder

If you're an autistic kid who likes dinosaurs, you are likely very interested in dinosaurs. Very, *very* interested. You will come to know all the names, all the facts, everything pertinent to their existence and extinction. As you accumulate this knowledge it feels somehow practical and *valuable*, and hence rewarding, as though there is an imperative driving you forward to accumulate and organize the knowledge. It's like assembling the final few pieces of a complicated puzzle, and it generates a similar satisfaction as those pieces fall into place.

For me, it has been computers for most of my life. I wandered into a Radio Shack store in about 1979, when I was 11, and saw my very first computer. It was not connected, as the staff had not yet figured out how to set it up. Being somewhat precocious, I asked whether they might let me play with it if I could manage to set it up. On a lark, they said, "Sure kid, have a shot," and ten minutes or so later I had it up and running. This endeared me to the manager, Brian, so much so that every Thursday night and Saturday morning I would ride my bike down to the store. I'd type in my crude BASIC programs, and they were kind enough to indulge my incessant tinkering on their expensive computer.

That level of autistic obsession really seems to know no bounds unless those bounds are somehow imposed upon the individual, at least when the person is still young. My parents had taught me not to "wear out my welcome" with people, but that didn't apply to computers. Had it been up to me I would have spent every free moment there. One memory remains very clear: at some point, the manager needed the machine for some official store business and told me I'd need to free it up for his use. As a kid, particularly when stressed or intimidated, my affect could be a little flat and my delivery a little dry--then as now, it can be hard to know when I'm kidding. When I replied to his demand by saying, "I'm going to save my work," he was somewhat taken aback, and rhetorically wanted to know,

"Are you telling me or asking me?" He thought perhaps I was kidding him.

Here is where, in retrospect, I feel a bit like the oblivious autistic kid I guess that I was: as I so often did with adults, I took him literally. I *wasn't* kidding, and yet I wasn't being obstinate. I was merely being accurate--I just needed to save my file, and I was letting him know that. The social nicety of deference to an adult was lost upon me, and so I replied, without a hint of being a smartass: "I'm telling you."

He didn't quite know what to say, other than "OK, then..." as he shook his head, turning to walk away while I busily fumbled with a blank audio cassette to save my work. Such misunderstandings where I completely misread the intent or meaning of other people would turn out to be common in my life.

## High School

If you want to know what the worst period of any autistic person's life has been, high school is usually a safe bet. You won't always be right, of course, but the odds are in your favor. My own high school experience, however, would turn out to be a little different than most.

As I approached high school age, my mom learned of a special "gifted" program being launched in our city; the top 20 applicants would be selected based on IQ testing and then subjected to a rigorous academic curriculum designed specifically for them. My testing went well. With my application accepted, that autumn I found myself amongst kindred spirits: other "freaks and geeks" such as myself. Almost all of us were weird in our own way and would have had trouble fitting into mainstream school. I would estimate that about one-third to one-half of the twenty kids were on the spectrum, though only one young man seemed more affected with potential autism symptoms than me. Coincidentally he also seemed the smartest, as so often seems to be the case, with the "severity" of symptoms appearing to linearly track intellect.

If it seems surprising that no one noticed that up to half of these hyper-smart kids were exhibiting signs of autism, remember that this was 1982 -- still six years before the movie *Rain Man* was released and a solid decade before Asperger's would even be introduced as a term. So "mild" autism symptoms just were not something educators and healthcare professionals were on the lookout for.

The gifted program provided what was perhaps my first major diagnostic clue in the autism puzzle, but we would all miss it at the time: aptitude testing. Each of us in the class was rigorously tested in several ways to best determine where our aptitude lay. When the results came in, my future careers were to be:

- Chicken Farmer
- Mortician

Since neither future was in the slightest way compelling to me, neither my parents nor the school placed much weight on the results, but they are interesting now since people in those professions spend very little time socially interacting with other people. Perhaps a career working alone with the deceased (or with chickens) is no more surprising than the career I did ultimately pick--working alone with a machine!

Unfortunately, the attrition rate for the gifted program was high; kids dropped out of the program rapidly and within a few years there wasn't a sufficient quorum of us left to form a class. We were dispersed and mainstreamed back into the general population, for better or worse. In my own case, it was for the worse.

I dropped out of high school entirely shortly thereafter. I was 17.

# From 7-Eleven to Microsoft

## New Workers at Freshly Unemployed Prices

When you suddenly need a job and you lack even a high school diploma, your choices can be limited. Faced with this dilemma myself, I drove my 1969 Pontiac down to my local 7-Eleven and filled out an application. After a couple of weeks of training, I was a proud new graveyard* cashier for 7-Eleven on South Albert in Regina, Saskatchewan, Canada, about as remote and lonely a place as you can imagine.

---

* The Eleven PM to Seven AM shift

The demands placed on the graveyard cashier, at least in those days, were significant, and keeping that position staffed relied on a steady stream of people that were quite smart but that must have had trouble finding a "better" job -- perhaps they each had interesting backgrounds or gaps in their education as I did.

Each night all the controlled inventory (cigarettes, lottery tickets, gasoline, and so on) must be fully accounted for. You literally go so far as to dip the in-ground fuel tanks with a 30-foot wooden pole to measure the fuel level change against the day's sales. The first night I attempted this, I released the pole letting it fall down into the hole, then re-grasped it as it was descending, which sent an explosion of wooden slivers into my now-freezing hands. You learn to wear gloves in a hurry.

The entire store, including the fridges and freezers, must be cleaned and restocked. All the bookkeeping is completed by the graveyard shift worker and rationalized against what cash and merchandise are actually present in the store. It's quite an extensive and impressive system, clearly evolved over decades to prevent losses from theft and embezzlement.

It seemed that I was especially well suited to working on detail-oriented tasks, entirely alone, into the wee hours of the morning. For me, it is hard to know where simple introversion ends and my autism begins, and in some ways, they seem inextricably connected, though that is hardly universal to people with autism. But I did *not* miss working with people for those hours, and I enjoyed the quiet and isolation.

I am also very task-oriented -- I like to work on one clearly defined and delineated task with maximum intensity for as long as it takes to complete it, and then I move on to something else. The night shift was comprised of a series of well-defined, detail-oriented, and sometimes challenging tasks that needed to be executed alone: in that sense, it was almost perfect for me.

Although by and large the store was quiet in the early morning hours, there was still the occasional customer, and being a cashier with autism can be difficult; the ebullience expected can be difficult to muster on command and even harder to maintain for an entire shift. Depending on my mood and how busy the store was, the few random customers that would wander in could be an annoyance or a reprieve. This process of being "on," known as masking, is covered in more detail in its own chapter.

Armed robberies were also a periodic threat, and after my second or third, one of the more astute police officers noted from the paperwork that I was technically too young, at only 17, to be working the night shift alone. And so ended my 7-Eleven career.

## The Teenage Epiphany

My next job found me in a large warehouse at the rear of a paint store; having grown up in and around my dad's family hardware store I was knowledgeable about paint, and it was thus a good fit for me. In simpler times, perhaps I could have lived my life out working in the back of a paint or hardware store. It's complex work, with paint bases and formulas and colorants and lots of rules and details to be mastered. I certainly felt at home.

But then, one day as I was in the back mixing a batch a thought came to me: *Next time around, I'll do life differently.*

As the implications of that thought sunk in -- there are no "do-overs," no "next times" -- I was stunned. I recognized immediately that my life wasn't on a great track and that I wanted to fix it. I wasn't sure how, but I knew something had to fundamentally change. And soon.

Faced with this major inflection point in my life, I did what any reasonable young man in his early 20s would do -- I went back to my local high school, sat down with the principal, and talked my way back in!

## Back to School

As surreal as being a grown adult in high school was, it was also brief: in only one semester I had completed enough credits to obtain my diploma. From there I went directly to the "Adult Entry Program" at my local university and enrolled. I would spend one semester in remedial classes to catch up on missing prerequisites and then college would begin in earnest.

One might imagine that by now I would have learned that being a good student takes significant effort, but I continued to coast my first semester, missing classes, and skipping homework. Then, one time after missing a few days in a row, I returned to discover the professor handing back a midterm exam -- one that I had not written! Apparently, I had skipped class that day. Although it would not lead to me failing the class (and as a remedial class it would not affect my overall grade,) it did require a "mercy pass" on the part of the instructor to get me through. The approach I'd been following all along simply wasn't working. I had the right goals now but evidently I still lacked the right approach.

As I think it might be for many people, the fundamental shift in how I went about things came with the realization that I was not going to school because I *had* to. No one was *making* me go. I was there of my own accord, for my own purposes and reasons. This understanding completely transformed the way I went about school; from that point forward, I treated it as something I wanted for myself, and I worked accordingly. By the end of my next semester, I was on the academic Dean's List, and I would graduate with Great Distinction from the Honors program four years later.

## The Food Court

During the summer break of my third year in 1992, I was working for the local phone company, doing network installation and troubleshooting. On my way to the mall food court for lunch, I stopped at a bookstore and picked up a copy of *Hard Drive: Bill Gates and the Making of the Microsoft Empire*, by James Wallace.

Traditionally, I had not been a fan of Microsoft, thinking them to be the 800-pound gorilla of the computer industry. But as I read the book, which was written in journalistic fashion, my perception gradually shifted. I became enthralled by the stories of the incredible people and the amazing projects at Microsoft. By the end of the book, I knew immediately -- and with great certainty -- what it was that I wanted to do with my life, and where I wanted to be.

The only problem was that Microsoft was a thousand miles away in another country in Redmond, Washington, USA, and I was sitting in a food court in Regina, Canada. How to go from one to the other?

In addition to working each summer to generate some income, I had also been writing and selling "shareware" software for the Amiga computer, a Microsoft competitor. Along the way, the users of my software would fill out and return the little blue registration cards that were common in the day, so I began searching through the hundreds of them to locate *anyone* with a Microsoft email address. Eventually, I found one.

## Microsoft Internship

That one card with its Microsoft email address turned out to be a customer named Alistair Banks; he promptly responded to my message. After some pleasantries were exchanged and I explained my situation he gave me the greatest gift you can give to an aspiring graduate: the contact info of a Microsoft development manager actively hiring new engineers! The fact that they could see my work before even speaking to me helped immensely -- as this, in turn, led to a telephone screening which then led to a live interview in Redmond. That grueling series of all-day interviews was rewarded with the summer internship during my senior year of college.

In June 1993 I ventured down to Microsoft for my four-month internship, going in with what might be best described as "full heads-down autism mode" on the projects assigned to me. I was entirely focused on and obsessed with the set of challenges before me. You might expect that they assign "token" projects to the young interns, but at Microsoft they had me working on MS-DOS itself, adding core features like CD-ROM support to their billion-dollar baby. Any failures would have serious consequences--and not for myself alone.

Fortunately, I turned in a worthy performance. From a technical standpoint, I met and then exceeded my goals, even taking on additional work items. On my review, however, I took a few dings for social and personal interactions with managers and coworkers. As was to become a pattern in my life, many people assumed I was grumpy until they truly got to know me, and the few that chose not to often "flipped a bit"* on me, assuming the sometimes-flat façade of autism was all that lay below the surface.

Had I known at the time that I had autism, or had someone advised me, I might have undertaken an attempt to mitigate some of the negative impacts. As we will see in much greater detail in the chapter Employment, there are many specific considerations to having a smoothly functioning workspace when people on the spectrum are involved. I knew none of that yet.

---

* "Flipping a bit" on someone at Microsoft meant deciding that someone is a particular way -- lazy, dumb, annoying, grouchy, etc. -- and then never revisiting that decision. I believe in some cases this is an example of "bracketing", discussed later.

I was as oblivious to the problems as I sometimes was to other people's emotions, and in some cases, it would take decades before I became fully aware of these significant liabilities.

# Coming to America

## Border Issues at the Border

A few months after my internship ended, I returned to Saskatchewan to finish university, where I had been dating a girl named Nicole for several years, since my return to high school. I was eager to propose but wanted to make sure I had a good job beforehand, and so I spent a lot of time waiting and hoping the phone would ring with a call from Microsoft.

Mid-semester, the call came in: Microsoft offered me a full-time position upon my graduation from college, complete with full benefits and -- better yet -- stock options. I think I likely accepted before I even knew what it paid in salary! Holding the phone while sitting on my bed down in the partially finished basement of my parents' nine-hundred square-foot house in Saskatchewan, I was so excited at being selected that I "forgot" to negotiate.

Later, when the UPS delivery drivers went on strike, I would learn that I perhaps *should* have pushed for more base salary, as at $35K per year I was earning significantly less than the average delivery driver--but ultimately the stock options would more than compensate[*]!

The final months of school flew by as I prepared to graduate and head off to the United States. I proposed marriage to my high school sweetheart and studied for final exams, which took place just before Christmas. I then headed down to the Seattle suburbs to find an apartment and start work at Microsoft, planning my return for the spring to officially graduate with the rest of my class.

On what was the Memorial Day long weekend down in the United States, I returned to Canada for a few of the busiest days of my life: my graduation ceremony was on Friday, after which we would load my fiancé's belongings into the back of a mover's van in advance of getting married on Saturday--a big family ceremony--before emigrating together to the United States on Monday!

My bride and I said goodbye to the movers bearing all our belongings and headed for the airport; upon landing at the US Customs entry point, however, I was pulled aside into the big glass room for additional questioning. After reviewing my application, with my new bride looking on from afar, the immigration officer started yelling at me, turning red, and waving his arms. He was very upset and animated, and from her vantage point it was clear to her that we were being denied

---

[*] According to the New York Times, Microsoft's 1986 initial public offering would ultimately create some 12,000 millionaires before I would even start my job there.

entry--my Microsoft dreams were crashing down around us right then and there.

What she didn't know, because she couldn't hear, was that he had already long since approved my work visa. He was *actually* upset because their copy of Microsoft Word was printing a blank page at the end of every one of their documents--it was wasting paper and he wanted it fixed. I did my best to help configure their page margins before we were released to our new life in America!

## Social Training Revisited

My wife, Nicole, and I moved to Seattle in 1994, at the peak of the grunge music scene. Although we lived out in the Seattle suburbs near the Microsoft office parks, weekends would take us and a core group of friends from the company to venture downtown into the city. We hit clubs such as the Fenix Underground, a new world for me, with new experiences, and new people drawn from diverse backgrounds. Live music was the standard and we danced to an odd Seattle mix of reggae, soca, rock, and grunge.

Some experts argue on behalf of specific social training for people on the spectrum in order to improve their level of functioning or to expand the number of social situations in which they are comfortable. Regardless of where you stand on formalizing the process, I don't think there can be any argument that both people *with and without* autism benefit from expanding their horizons, and I was doing it weekly.

Not only was I learning to socialize with new crowds, but I was also learning to socialize with a new style of person I hadn't had a lot of exposure to: the kind of openly hyper-intelligent and driven people that I was surrounded with daily at work now, regardless of their spectrum status. About half of our friends were programmers, like me, and the other half were in finance and HR like my wife, and thus it was a good mix socially.

As a Canadian transplant, I jumped at the chance to see a favorite Canadian band, the Tragically Hip, when they came to perform at a nearby club. Whereas the Hip were popular enough in Canada, playing occasional large stadium concerts in Toronto, they were still obscure enough in the USA to be playing small venues. They were scheduled to play at a small dance club called Under the Rail, making it a huge opportunity, and so off we went!

## There's an Autistic Guy in the Mosh Pit!

I took a group of American friends, mostly from Microsoft, to see the band. We were an eclectic group: a Canadian programmer, my Ukrainian wife Nicole from finance, a Scottish tester with triple citizenship, a New York Jewish transplant from HR, my Indian racquetball nemesis, and the future CTO of AOL, who could not be cajoled into the mosh pit at any price.

His reluctance to enter the pit likely made him the wiser of us, as I'd never been in one either, but the opening act was still performing, and the crowd was still somewhat sedate. It looked safe enough. I made my way to center stage, but then the main act suddenly debuted and the crowd's energy instantly spiked, taking me by surprise. People in the pit started slamming to the left and slamming to the right, and thanks to my less-than-athletic rhythm and dance ability, I went down almost immediately. My glasses went flying in some random direction, and I was briefly in genuine fear of being trampled underfoot. I need not have worried, as a group of people quickly scooped me up, held me aloft in the air, and my eyeglasses surfed the crowd back to me, being passed person to person until they reached me. Say what you will about mob mentality, it was pretty friendly to me that night. New "Crowd Surfing Achievement" unlocked*? Check!

## Microsoft Culture and Autism

Even if a good deal of Microsoft culture was formed around the quirks and personalities of many people that likely had autism in some form, during the years that I worked there, it was still so new as a concept that it was little talked about. If anything, the programmers bifurcated into "geeks" and "nerds," with the "geeks" more likely to be on the spectrum. That's about as far as we bothered to self-identify, but both groups were well represented. There were a few people like Aaron, generally senior to me and hired well before me, who seemed more

> *"I think all tech people are slightly autistic."*
>
> Douglas Coupland, Microserfs

---

* In video game terminology, when a player completes some challenge for the first time, they are rewarded with the notification "Achievement Unlocked." I look at some social experiences in a similar way--completing as many new and different social experiences as I can for the sake of growth, building my repertoire of things done.

autistic by nature than I was, and of course, there were many more that were less so. If anything, our internal measure of whether a person had autism (or Asperger's as we then called it) was based on their communication and hygiene -- basic social metrics -- not any formal brain science!

Today, Microsoft reports that it attempts to recruit and hire people on the spectrum for reasons that we discuss in the chapter on Employment, but even in my day being on the spectrum could put you at a marked disadvantage during the interview process. That process usually began with a phone screen and as will be discussed later, I'm usually very uncomfortable on the phone.

In my experience, as job interview candidates, people on the spectrum often tend to give yes or no answers and do not go on waxing poetic at length about their past projects, even if they're impressive. We'd generally prefer that the person doing the interview ask detailed leading questions about those projects, and we will happily fill you in--but it doesn't always feel natural or relevant to bring any accomplishments up on our own. Essentially, we are sometimes not good advocates for our own hiring. As an example of how the details can obscure the greater goal, I might have worked on an amazing technical task two years ago, but if the product it yielded has since been superseded by a competitor, I would consider that achievement now pointless and perhaps not mention the work, even though it's entirely relevant to the hiring decision. I would likely let its current obsolescence override its relevance because I have poor central coherence, something we shall explore in more detail later. Put simply, it means I fail to see "the big picture" when

I'm focused on details. Where others can see the forest, I see only trees, and sometimes, just the leaves and branches.

For all its potential sins, one beauty of the Microsoft interview process back in the rough-and-tumble-1990s, however, was "whiteboard coding." You would be given a whiteboard, a marker, and a simple programming problem--such as to reverse a linked list--and you had to write the code in the terse C++ programming language. This was an opportunity to sell your ability rather than selling your persona. It didn't matter what color or creed you were, what gender, whether you were handsome or ugly, nothing mattered when your face was to the board. For a brief few minutes, at least, only the code would matter. A good interviewing programmer can almost "mind meld" another programmer when they're spilling out code. They see what you write, they know what you're thinking and why. If (and how) your code handles potential contingencies and errors, that tells them all that needs to be known about how bold and pedantic you are. To be honest, as a hiring manager, whatever else you tell me about yourself means very little after watching you code.

Jumping head-first into the very demanding Microsoft interview process would represent a change in anyone's normal daily routine and can be more than a little stressful, to say the least. Combine that with the stress of traveling to visit the campus, the forced socializing in the evenings, the endless series of in-person interviews, and it really can be a perfect storm for someone on the spectrum. In the course of my career, I personally interviewed hundreds of candidates and hired dozens but only saw one or two meltdowns myself. And I only had one of my own.

When I had been at Microsoft for about five years, two major teams with similar mandates were merged. We had been internal competitors, and now we were peers, working hand in hand. However, as my job had previously been to fix the defects coming out of the other team, and because I likely wasn't always as gracious with my feedback as I might have been, some mistrust and animosity still lingered between us in both directions.

One day, I had to take my design for a new software interface to be reviewed by their senior developer. In those days, as a new programmer at Microsoft, you might start out as a Level 10, with the career ladder progressing all the way up to Level 15 -- which is what Chris was. If we were gorillas, I might be bigger, but he would have been the silverback. I'd always liked Chris personally, and while he wasn't a technical hero of mine, I absolutely respected his ability. So, when he rejected my first design, I was a little disappointed. When he rejected the second revision a few days later, I was outright hurt by it. I went back to the drawing board to rework my design into something that would really impress him. But when that third version (which I was certain was getting needlessly close to perfection) was also rejected, the frustration became overwhelming. It felt unjust, unfair, and not realistic. As I stood in his office after investing days of intense effort into something that was being rejected for what I *believed* were purely personal reasons, I was about to break down. It seemed there was nowhere left to go logically: I turned red, no doubt looked like I was about to cry, and felt an overwhelming need to flee. It's difficult to explain why, but perhaps when the "fight" reflex is constrained only "flight" can remain, and it can feel very amplified*. I stayed silent for a few seconds, collected myself, and said the only words I could muster: "It feels like you're arguing for sport." It was true that it felt that way to me at the time, but with autism, it's hard to know the objective reality when it comes to certain emotional matters. Today I would absolutely *not* attempt to interpret his motives. More likely, I would simply ask for crisper feedback on exactly what he wanted to be done differently (i.e., how he would have done it himself), go back, and make that happen. Handling such matters is covered in more detail in the chapter on Employment.

By far the biggest misunderstanding, however -- one that came close to costing me my job along with potentially millions in stock options -- came soon after, and it too was complicated by my autism.

## Code on the Side

Computer programming, or coding, is my special interest. My love for writing code means that even while I was working at Microsoft, I still wrote code at home in my spare time at night and on weekends. One day, while driving through a neighborhood of new homes for sale, I saw a fellow outside his beautiful suburban home, which was for sale, washing his beautiful new red Corvette. I grabbed a color picture flyer from

---

* Children with autism often wander, bolt, or run off, and I wonder if the drive they feel in that moment is the same one I experience.

the sign box and took it home, cut out the picture of the house, and taped it to the side of my monitor. If I ever needed extra incentive to pursue my special interest, it would serve as inspiration while coding late into the night.

One example of software that began at home with me, and that you may have seen before, is the Windows Task Manager. I wrote the original in my den in 1994, intending to release it as a shareware utility, but when the more senior developers at work saw it, they wanted to include it with Windows itself. So, I agreed to donate it to the cause and add it to the Windows product, where it remains to this day (though substantially evolved from when I last touched it, of course). I received no compensation for it, nor did I ask for or expect any.

A second example can be found in ZIPFolders, which gives Windows the native ability to open and browse down inside a bundled zip file as if it were a complete hard drive of its own. Another case of shareware* code I wrote in my den, this one made it to full release, and it was finding its audience online via the fledgling World Wide Web.

Somehow a Windows product manager at Microsoft stumbled across the utility and decided that it, too, belonged in the operating system as part of Windows. To that end she called me at home early one morning before I'd left for work, to explain that Microsoft wanted to purchase the program from me for

---

* With shareware, a user typically downloads a free trial or time-limited evaluation version, and if they find the software useful, they can then mail-order or purchase a full licensed copy online.

inclusion in Windows--would I be willing to discuss it? I offered to stop by her office that morning, which seemed to alarm her--she demurred and said I should talk to Microsoft Travel, which confused the heck out of me. *Why would I schedule a travel visit to Microsoft when I worked there every day? I lived only a few blocks away!*

It turned out, after some uncomfortable back and forth, that this product manager had no idea that I worked at Microsoft, just as she did! She had merely researched, tracked down, and cold-called the author of the program--who happened to be me--at home to explore an acquisition.

In the end, my options were quite limited. If I did not sell my program to Microsoft, they would develop their own version or buy a competing one, and I'd have to stop selling mine or quit my day job--I couldn't just continue selling mine in competition with my own employer once they had entered the same market! And so, I cheerfully accepted their first, best, and only offer. My first big acquisition in the software industry would be from my own employer. It wasn't enough to buy the house in the flyer, but it was enough to buy a (used) red Corvette like the one I'd coveted all those months before. But that's when ZIPFolders almost cost me my job.

## Hiroshi

Because I had been writing software on the side all through college and planned to continue doing so while at Microsoft, I had been careful to get very specific permission to do so on my employment agreement when I was initially hired. Microsoft was surprisingly accommodating of such matters, with the one exception being if your "moonlighting" were too closely related to your day job. If, for example, you knew trade secret information that the public did not have access to, you obviously couldn't take advantage of it. If there were any questions as to whether the side project was too closely related to your day job, the permission would have to come from very high on up -- perhaps a Senior Vice President or above.

My ZIPFolders app was not the only one out there like it, and when one of my competitors discovered that I worked at Microsoft, they took great objection to it and somehow contacted a developer in my own division who was, at the time, quite senior to me. The competitor protested vociferously that it was unfair for me to be competing with them while I also worked at Microsoft. The internal developer in question -- we'll call him Hiroshi -- agreed, and he undertook a personal mission to see that I was made an example of. Although we knew each other, he did not come to see me; he went directly to HR to have me fired immediately.

That news promptly cascaded down to Mark, my direct manager, and Bob, the most senior developer on our team. Earning my eternal gratitude, they went to bat for me, and they both lost a great deal of sleep over the next few days trying to save my job. Although I believed that I had my ducks in a row with the proper prior signed permission, Hiroshi made the argument that the permission did not come from high enough up in the company because he believed that my project was too closely related to my Microsoft work. My livelihood -- including all my stock options -- hung in the balance!

This is where my autism entered the picture in full force. I am very, very bad at just letting things play out on their own. By nature, I am a fixer, and as a fixer with autism, it is incredibly difficult for me to be in a bad situation and do nothing about it, such as to simply wait it out. I need to be constantly engaged in trying to actively resolve the most important problem in my life at any given time -- waiting *never* feels like a viable option. Sometimes waiting is thrust upon me, and that can be very difficult.

If you have a child with autism who demands that whatever problem they are facing be solved *immediately*, rest assured that I understand the instinct. It's one that sometimes gets the better of me, unfortunately.

Rather than letting the matter run its natural course, I decided to force the issue by escalating it. I contacted my Senior Vice President as well as Microsoft's top attorney -- the general counsel of the entire company -- and asked for a ruling. In one of the shortest but sweetest emails I've ever received, the answer came back the next morning: "I have no problem with this." In the Microsoft vernacular of the day, I was "golden," thereby rendering Hiroshi impotent.

I believe some people with autism tend to hold grudges because their social system can be so rigorously rule based. In many pop culture portrayals of autism, such as *Rain Man* and *Big Bang Theory*, we see people with autism literally maintaining paper journals of injuries and slights committed by others over time*. Just as a person may never be able to eat a particular food after becoming sick on it, anyone who wrongs me maliciously will be flagged permanently (just like a bad food!), unless and until something changes. I count myself lucky in that I only have one mortal enemy, and it's Hiroshi, whom I have not seen in person in more than twenty-five years and who may not even recall the incident after all this time.

## MemTurbo

Around the turn of the millennium, late one Friday a coworker and I were skimming through some of the latest new shareware releases online when I came across a program intended to make more memory available on your computer. It seemed genius, particularly back in those days when memory was very expensive and every byte was precious but unfortunately, the program was quite poorly made. I could see the potential of the program, but it needed to be done right. Such opportunities are made for me: I am at my best doing a great version of someone else's OK idea. In other words, not unlike Microsoft itself, perhaps, I am an excellent "fast follower."

All these years later, I can still visualize exactly where we were standing when I turned to my coworker, and in a burst of bravado combined with raw enthusiasm exclaimed, "I'm going to buy myself a new car!" There are times with autism where a

---

* This devotion to tracking past hurts may not be far from the truth, but most of us don't require the journal to write them down in. We just remember forever.

thought wants to come out that really should be suppressed by a filter: things that a neurotypical person might think, but never say. Tourette's is often comorbid with autism -- while being different and separate from it -- but I think many people on the spectrum who do not officially count Tourette's as their condition, do experience narratives that they later wish had stayed internal!

Regardless, I knew that -- done properly -- this program would likely sell very well. I went home after work and got down to business that night, cranking out a rough draft of the core functionality over the weekend.

In the coming weeks, I released the program to the internet; I titled it MemTurbo. Sales began to trickle in, and eventually, I was selling about a half dozen copies a day. By now we had two children at home, and though a twenty-dollar per-copy profit wasn't an enormous amount of money, it sure helped with the diapers and baby formula and so on!

In those days, back when my wife and I were recent transplants to the USA, we still celebrated Canadian thanksgiving at home, which is a couple of months earlier than the traditional American holiday. Just as I sat down to my traditional dinner of turkey and maple syrup, the phone rang -- I was about to ignore it but for some reason picked up the line. On the other end was a fellow named Matt from McAfee software -- where they weren't celebrating the holiday -- and they wanted to help promote my software on their own website in exchange for a cut of the sale price. It was a no-risk deal and I jumped at the chance! As much as I dislike the phone, it's true that many of my opportunities have come through it, so it's a good thing that using the telephone is one of those things I force myself to do.

Soon MemTurbo was selling up to thirty copies a day through McAfee's website, and I realized that if advertising on one website was generating those kinds of sales, what if I advertised more broadly? I had never purchased ad space before, always relying on word of mouth to promote my products, but if it worked on the McAfee website, odds are it might work elsewhere as well. I promptly set up an account with a large internet advertising agency and created a few of my very first banner advertisements.

I uploaded my ads to their automated system along with my credit card information to pay for running the advertisements. Instead of just one website, now my ads could run across tens of thousands of sites. Foolishly, I did not even *think* to set a limit on how many advertisements would run each day, and when I came back the next day to check on progress, I discovered that I had spent *ten thousand dollars* in a single day on advertising! My thoughts immediately turned to how I was going to explain this utterly boneheaded mistake to my wife.

Hoping against hope, I went to check the sales report and see how many copies had sold based on those advertisements; perhaps the revenue from whatever sales were generated would at least help offset my advertising costs. It would turn out that they more than did so!

I discovered that I had sold over *one thousand copies* in that single day! Through bundling and upsells, the average sale price approached forty dollars for a daily total of over forty thousand dollars -- in a day! I checked and rechecked and triple-checked everything, to ensure I wasn't seeing things, and I was not: it really had made thirty thousand dollars of profit in a single day. I was truly stunned. The biggest sales days, such as when an upgrade was available, would peak at over one hundred thousand dollars per day. This was all before considering any expenses such as the advertising itself, of course.

*Disk duplicators in my closet, 1999*

Sales increased over the next few weeks until the average daily total passed 1,440 per day, an important mental milestone for me because it signified an average of one copy per minute over 24 hours. People with autism often have a fascination with numbers, and for me, certain numbers carry a significant psychological impact. The numeric totals, for some reason, really served to add emotional content. Prime numbers, large round numbers, the year of your birth--these can feel important to people on the spectrum for reasons that are truly difficult to articulate. When there were 1,440 sales in a day, the day felt complete, square, and whole somehow because one sale could be fit into each minute. If there were only 1,439 sales, it would be like a boat missing a tiny fraction of its hull: incomplete.

I had rigged up the computer in the den to play a loud, live *$Ka-Ching!* cash-drawer sound every time a sale occurred, day or night -- and as Nicole and I listened for it, it became a background feature of our home lives in those years. Occasionally there would be a lull with no sales, and that would prompt me to check the systems to make sure everything was running smoothly. Sometimes they would come in bursts -- *KaChing! KaChing! KaChing!* It was invigorating and exciting for us.

In a way, because I had written all of it (the software, the marketing, and even the documentation), every aspect of the program down to the smallest detail was a complete reflection of me, and so every sale became a personal vindication: a tiny affirmation of my worth each time the bell rang[*].

---

[*] I bet every time he heard a bell ring, Pavlov thought about feeding his dogs.

I developed a complete online store, point of sale system, and credit card processing pipeline to handle the orders. In the early days, each order's credit card payment was processed by having the computer dial out – by modem, no less! -- to contact the bank's credit card gateway. The orders would be batched up during the day and I would process them in the evening. If there were a thousand orders, it meant the computer had to dial the phone and connect the modem one thousand times. When we were visiting my in-laws, the business traveled with me by laptop. My teenage sister-in-law was none too pleased to have the phone tied up for hours each evening and the incessant sound of the modem processing orders was music to my ears only.

Combined with a live web reporting system that came to be known as "Day So Far", my brain fell into sync with the operation of the business. In a very real sense, the business, and more specifically managing the minute-to-minute optimization of the sales funnel, became my new autistic "special interest." I was tuned into the operation of the business in the way a dedicated mechanic might be in tune with a car's engine as he adjusts the carburetor by feel and sound and smell. If the slightest thing started to go wrong, I could sense it from the data and react accordingly. I fine-tuned the sales pipeline constantly based on the metrics we were observing.

Sometimes I would awaken with a start in the middle of the night with an idea, and I would wander into the spare bedroom to tweak the advertisement or web page in question so that it could collect data for the rest of the night. I'd return to sleep and by morning I'd know if the change had helped or hurt sales.

I must imagine that examples like this serve to illustrate how challenging it must be to compete with an entrepreneur that has autism. If nothing else, we're fully dedicated to our task.

The sales rate of about one per minute would be sustained for years, until we had reached our millionth customer, then continuing from there. Waking up to find that you're selling thousands of copies of your computer program a day feels exactly like you imagine it might--it's like winning the lottery every morning. It's also an *incredible* amount of pressure not to mess it up! Imagine knowing your lottery number had won but that you were not entirely certain where you had left the ticket: it's an odd combination of exhilaration and stress.

In the early days, the biggest challenge was simply keeping up. I would work all day at Microsoft and then come home to potentially several hundred emails that I had to work through, including email orders and returns and a ton of technical support. Plus, because we were producing our own disks and packages and mailers, I had to make hundreds of copies of the diskette every day, package them with instructions, put postage on and mail them. There was just no way I could keep up, even with Nicole pitching in almost full time. We recruited her sister Jacquie and other family members to jump into the fray, responding to customer emails, even enlisting neighborhood kids in the production of the disks, mailers, and instructions. All of this took place in my tiny ten-foot square den at home, and when it spilled forth and took over our kitchen table, we began to look for office space.

# We're Going to Transition You Out of the Portfolio

Early one morning I received a call from Visa/Mastercard. They had noticed that we were doing over a million dollars a month in sales*, and they were worried. The World Wide Web was still a new and novel concept at the time, and more traditional businesses like Visa were concerned because our customers were purchasing software licenses, not brick and mortar style goods. The card issuers viewed the monthly totals in outstanding credit card charges as effectively a temporary loan to my company. They were particularly worried that a small company like mine could simply close shop one day and leave them holding the bag on all the returns. It was a lot of risk for them to carry: if my website disappeared overnight, they could be on the hook for a million dollars' worth of refunds to angry customers before anyone even knew I was gone or where I went.

That morning they called me to explain that their risk management department had decided that they were going to "transition me out of the portfolio." I struggled to determine exactly what that meant in practical terms until I figured out that it was just a euphemism for: "You won't be able to accept

---

* With sales volume numbers that large, the profit margins are paramount, and such a business either prints money or hemorages it. Each month would produce hundreds of thousands of dollars in either profits or losses, all depending on the effectiveness of the advertising I created. It was a feast or famine, high-stress business.

credit cards anymore. Period." When 100% of your business is done by credit card, that's a problem. A *big* problem!

I went back and forth with the account representative, but there seemed to be no hope of changing his mind. Finally, in a move of desperation plucked from thin air, I suggested a radical way for them to remove almost all their risk: I would simply give *them* a million dollars cash, to hold onto "just in case," as collateral. At this point, cash flow was the least of our problems, and I had to park it somewhere anyway. After a few days of discussions on the details and one very big deposit later, we were set, and the business was free to continue rolling along. Over time Visa/Mastercard reduced the size of the bond and eventually, after a few years of working together, they waived the requirement entirely and returned the money. Had I not stumbled across this idea while flailing on the telephone to keep the company alive, the entire enterprise might have ended before it had truly even got started!

## Quitting my Day Job

I loved my day job and I loved Microsoft -- it had been my calling. I had gone to school for it, left my birth nation, relocated, and built a new life around it. But there was simply no way I could continue there; the side business had grown too lucrative to ignore and I could not do both well. The distraction of the side business was impacting my performance at Microsoft noticeably; the simple economics, combined with the reality of how much work was involved, meant that my time there was coming to an end. I undertook one final major project at Microsoft -- the addition of product keys and software licensing to Windows -- just to prove, as much to myself as to anyone, that I could still perform at a high level*.

Then I left. First, I took a three-month sabbatical to find out for certain if it was truly what I wanted to do, and when those three months were up, I put in my notice right at the start of 2003. I had spent ten very rewarding years in the operating systems division, and Windows XP and Server 2003 would be my last products.

Only later would I realize how hard leaving Microsoft was on my self-esteem. So much of my self-worth and value had come from being selected out of Saskatchewan to work there--once taken away, a large void was left in my psyche.

## My Own Mini Microsoft

Without the distraction of a day job, I was able to turn my full attention to my own software business. We secured office space, computers, and more staff. I hired Brad, a talented business attorney, to become our company president and to run the day-to-day operations. We added new products and new markets and Brad did a wonderful job of all the business stuff that I would have been terrible at, such as the minutiae of ensuring compliance, savings plans, benefits, and so on.

I undertook to entice some of the very best people that I had worked with at Microsoft to come and join me, and the

---

* That super-long and annoying "Product Key" that you must enter into Windows to prove you have a purchased license? That's my doing!

company began to grow. At its peak, we had thirty-five employees and total revenue of over one hundred million dollars from more than two million unique customers. Even so, I hand-wired and crimped the terminals on all 70 telephone and ethernet connections, installed and programmed the phone and alarm systems by myself, and much more. It remained a basement operation even as it grew.

This habit of doing it all myself can be a blessing and a curse. On the one hand, I've acquired a great deal of skill and experience across a wide set of topics that I otherwise would not have, but is it the highest and best use of my time really to be crimping phone wires? This trait of refusing to delegate would come to have far more dire consequences than mere phone lines, however. If there is one primary mistake that I made while running my

> "They're good at coming up with ideas, identifying market niches, creatively engineering something from nothing, selling it to other people and pulling together a team that's motivated to follow them," he says. [Those] who do well surrender day-to-day management once the company is self-sustaining or sell it and move on. Those who keep doing it all, he warns, usually self-destruct."

*Entrepreneur Magazine, June 2006*

55

own company, it was that I underestimated the number of things that other people would do as well as, or better than, I could.

I believe that the lack of central coherence that often accompanies autism caused me to focus far too much on the tiny details rather than on the big picture--what color of wire goes into which slot rather than overall company strategy. I could have hired someone to do that wiring and perhaps opened for business a few days earlier, more than offsetting the cost of a professional. This was not limited to phone cables, however--it was true of the way I approached most of what our company did, including software development. I had hired away two of my most talented coworkers from Microsoft, but I did not give them the autonomy to simply make things happen. Rather than describe *what* we needed doing and letting them run with that information, I became overly involved in the details of *how* things were to be done. To a lesser extent, I followed this same approach on the business side as well. Like many founders in general, and many on the autism spectrum, I had a hard time letting go of the details.

## The First Million Widgets is the Hardest

With the Company being focused on the online sales of utility software, my main task was not in the writing of the software, but rather in the design, testing, measuring, and optimization of online advertisements. In reality, any reasonably talented engineer could have written any of our popular software products, but only a few people could sell them profitably in high quantities, and I seemed to be one of them. But why?

Designing such advertisements means creating two primary pieces of creative: the small advertisement (such as a banner) that the user initially sees and clicks on, and the landing page that they are taken to visit in their web browser when they do. It is the job of the landing page to convince the consumer to part with their money by buying something, like hair gel, or to do something, like signing up for car insurance. Our landing pages convinced users to install a free trial version of our software that they could try it for up to thirty days without a credit card, totally anonymously. We just wanted you to *try* it, and we were confident there was a chance that you'd buy it once you had seen it in action. Statistically, for us to break even would require only perhaps one percent of visitors to purchase it in the end. If I could convince more than one percent, we'd make money--any less, and we'd rapidly lose it.

One might imagine that mindblindness would make it difficult if not impossible for someone with autism to be successful at designing marketing campaigns and creatives. After all, the whole process, it seemed to me, was based on imagining how the reader would interpret and react to the content. I had to simulate another brain within my own, forecasting whether the sales pitch would work.

Perhaps I was merely selling to myself and using my own mind as a proxy for the consumer, but in fact, our sales data indicated the demographic for our typical customer was not a technical person like me at all. Regardless of the reasons, I was very skilled at creating effective advertisement and landing pages, and we purchased literally billions of advertising impressions back in those years. Each month we would risk about a million dollars a month in speculative advertising, hoping to return more than that in direct-to-consumer sales. In those months that we did, we turned a healthy profit. But in months we did not, the cash burn was *very* fast.

I believe certain forms of higher functioning autism may lend themselves very well to the marketing field, as those who experience its symptoms spend so much of their regular mental energy in simulating other people's thoughts. Because a sense of what the other might be thinking doesn't come naturally, it becomes a much more mechanical and analytical process. Perhaps the practice and repetition of trying to anticipate what other people are thinking in response to information presented to them help build a core skill set that is related to or needed for successful marketing. That said, all the marketing material I've ever created is manifestly straightforward and unemotional--a logical explanation of why you'd be better off owning it than not[*]. I imagine I would be useless at marketing fashion, for example.

Fortunately, when it worked, it worked well, and we often doubled our investment each month. With a 30-day, no-questions-asked, toll-free, "just pick up the phone" return policy and a free trial version to test drive the product in advance, customer satisfaction ran well over ninety-nine

---

[*] It turns out I am very much a fan of the David Ogilvy style of advertising, which favors convincing exposition over merely an emotional headline… perhaps not a surprise!

percent. It had to, as the credit card agencies would fret mightily if the chargeback[*] ratio even approached one percent.

Although everyone crossed responsibilities somewhat, I ran the technical side of the business. Brad continued as our president. Allen, from Microsoft, ran the marketing side and my sister-in-law, Jacquie, moved down from Canada to run the sales department. By the summer of 2001, we held the "One-Millionth Customer" barbeque in my suburban backyard. The party went wonderfully until, in a strong foreshadowing of unexpected events to come, the lawn sprinklers burst into action in the middle of it!

## In Hot Water

Like many (but not all) people on the spectrum, I am a highly visual thinker. In fact, even if you tell me something non-visual, I might still remember whatever it was I was looking at anyway. For example, one time, rather than being at work worrying about my multi-million-dollar software business, I was at home demonstrating my poor central coherence by trying to fix the water heater. That's when the phone rang, and Brad gave me the news: the attorney general (AG) of Washington State was suing our business for consumer protection violations. That memory is forever locked to the image of the yellow energy guide sticker on the side of the water heater I was fixing. Just as emotional memories are often

---

[*] A chargeback is when the customer contacts the credit card company directly, rather than the selling merchant, for a refund.

frozen in time for the neurotypical, it seems visual memories are similarly saved away for me.

At first, I was only standing in a little hot water. I was soon about to be up to my knees in it. Everyone was about to see just how autistic I really was, and yet none of us yet knew it.

## The Laundry List

We finally received a copy of the lawsuit that the AG was planning to file--I was flabbergasted. It was a curious mix of a few genuine concerns and a dozen wild, unsubstantiated claims thrown in for good measure. Apparently, this is par for the course in legal matters: if they think X *might* be true, it's easier to claim X up front than to add it to the lawsuit later. As a result, the attorneys can tend to load cases up with a lot of speculative claims, and this was no exception. I didn't know it was standard procedure, and it derailed me.

In yet another example of poor central coherence, I became unduly concerned with the fact that the AG was asserting almost a dozen completely speculative claims when I should have been focusing on the one or two legitimate concerns that did have at least some merit. I could see only the claims I knew to be untrue and my mind couldn't get past them.

After some persistence, we managed to get the AG to at least meet on the phone to discuss the case. It was being handled by Audrey, an assistant attorney general (AAG) and as humorless a person as I can recall ever having met. Audrey made it clear that there was little point in even talking to her, as they "had all they needed" and weren't interested in settlement talks. I suppose it was all standard legal maneuvering, but it worked on me like an old case of "good cop-bad cop."

Brad, our attorneys, and I took part in a conference call with the AAG. I was starting to feel the pressure, and I let them know I wasn't pleased with their approach to the lawsuit by telling Audrey as much. I said, "You can't simply march into my business with a laundry list of a dozen things you think *might* be true …" At which point I was interrupted by my own attorney attempting to save me from myself. He said,

"No, no, no, no . . . it's not a laundry list, but . . ."

Apparently, you're not supposed to call a lawsuit a "laundry list." I know that now, but it didn't help me then. Audrey was not amused, and we would have only one remaining chance to meet with her before their suit was filed.

## But I'm a Big Boy!

At this point in the company's history, my wife Nicole had been running human resources and finance. As our family grew at home, she had transitioned most of her company responsibilities over to other executives, but she remained quite involved in day-to-day operations. When it came time to meet with the AAG, however, should I take my wife with me? It didn't involve her department, and other than her role as a shareholder, there was no compelling business reason for her to be there.

Beyond that, however, my wife is *great* with people. As discussed in the chapter on relationships, it's quite possible I was drawn to her in no small part to help compensate for my own rather ample shortcomings in that area. I wanted her there as the "Dave whisperer," someone who could act as an intermediary between my sometimes-detached demeanor and the human side of the AAG. It's not beyond imagination that my wife and Audrey could have sat down and worked it all out between them, becoming best friends and going on to exchange Pinterest stories about online advertising to this very day. I could also have used Nicole as a touchstone, a safe spot from which I could operate in the meeting. I'll never know for certain if it would have made a difference as ultimately, we decided as a team that I would go it alone with just Brad and our lead counsel.

We arrived at the offices of the attorney general and were given name stickers. I had once ruined a leather jacket with a similar sticker, so I put it on my leg instead, only to be chastised by my attorney: "Today is not the day to be a rebel, Dave." I didn't get the hint as well as I perhaps should have. This day would be all about perceptions, not facts.

The meeting was brief and unproductive. About halfway through I asked one of the AAG's attorneys for a tally of just how many of the millions upon millions of people who had used our software had actually complained to the attorney general. Perhaps the problems *were* bigger than I thought. When the answer came back as "four\*," I was stunned. All of this -- the stress, the expense, the sleepless nights -- because

---

\* I forget the precise number today, but it was a small number that surprised me. It could have been 2, or 37, or 13. But it wasn't many hundreds or thousands.

four people in several million had complained. The attorney general traditionally gets involved when hundreds or thousands of people complain about something, not *four*!

I said something to the effect of, "Surely, you must agree that if we were harming consumers in some way, more than four would have complained by now, would they not?" The answer came back that "some of the most insidious scams are the ones that the consumers are not even aware of." Thus, the number of complaints was irrelevant to them: their logic was flawless, impenetrable, and completely useless to me.

I was in over my head and *way* out of my element. Being the target of a lawsuit can be very problematic and stressful for someone on the spectrum, as so much of the legal maneuvering is based on negotiation, strategy, mindreading, and emotional nuances that are very hard for someone with autism to understand. I had no idea. I honestly thought that I would be able to talk, reason, explain, and "logic" my way through the matter like it was an engineering problem. It's not that I underestimated how serious the issue was, it was that I overestimated the value of analytical logic when it comes to legal matters.

Those matters might not make a lot of logical sense to a programmer, but I'm sure they make sense to a lawyer, and when you've got autism and are facing legal trouble, you need a lawyer who can manage both the case and your special needs. You are likely going to experience more angst, frustration, and worry than a neurotypical client, and you will benefit from an attorney who has a tableside manner compatible with helping you through that. I did not know that I had autism then and thought my own quirky needs were merely that. In contrast, if I needed an attorney today, I would rely on recommendations from friends that understood this aspect of the disorder. With the attorney in question, I would have had an initial informative discussion, covering something like the following:

"I have high-functioning autism, often known as Asperger's. As a result, I suffer from lower central coherence in that I often get bogged down in the details and can miss the big picture; I need you to help me stay focused on what's truly important in the case. I am unduly troubled by any inaccurate details even if they are not relevant. Help me look past them. I am particularly bad at adapting to unwanted and unexpected change, experiencing frustration easily when things do not seem to be going my way. I can become distracted and need encouragement to move through such hard moments. I also like to be personally involved and informed with the current state and details of the case more than others might, and I need you to balance those desires with what's practical."

I worked with our attorneys to try to see it from the other side so that I could have a sense of what was truly most important to the AG. It seemed there were two issues of primary concern: that our advertisements must not overstate risks to consumers using tone, color, verbiage, or other elements, and that the checkout page on our website complied with all applicable regulations.

## Breakin' the Law, Breakin' the Law

Most important was the style of advertisement – the color, tone, and text. We had dozens, if not hundreds, of different ads, and they would *all* need to be reviewed. Fortunately, most of them were quite basic, largely simple text content directed at getting the user to test drive and evaluate the product, not to make an actual purchase. In the end, we happily offered the attorney general our assurances on a more crisply defined set of standards for our ads going forward. Those changes didn't require us to make any big changes in the current ads, so the case really did not change the ongoing business in any material sense.

Our trial model also served to make this process much simpler, and because free trial/evaluation versions always existed for all our software, it was never really a high-pressure sale. The fact that the user could always try for up to a month before buying brought with it a certain level of confidence in the purchase.

In the end, the biggest problem was that we had a checkbox on our order page that was plain and obvious, but which defaulted to ON for standard postal shipping and handling. Being almost twenty years ago, people at the time were accustomed to their software coming on a CD or floppy disk, and so we defaulted to a disc in the mail rather than a digital-only download. This is because previously we had found that defaulting to a digital download meant that a week or two after an order was placed, we would receive angry calls from the customer who was expecting a disc to arrive in the mail. When we explained that they hadn't even ordered a physical disc, but that we could easily sell or send them one now, the normal response was to just cancel the order in frustration. Making the disc the delivery default avoided this frustration for the consumer. It made logical sense to me and seemed to make everyone happy -- everyone except Washington State, that is.

That's because, under Washington state law, our default of having the checkbox "checked" for the optional disc/download was illegal because it was considered "negative option billing" -- it required you to opt *out* of an optional expense (such as the shipping and handling) during a purchase. The law is the law, and we had broken it, even if unwittingly. To wrap it up we agreed to pay a penalty, most of which would be suspended based on our future compliance with the agreement (spoiler alert: we complied, of course!). We agreed to a stipulated judgment that defined where we had gone wrong and provided our assurances never to repeat such mistakes. It also gave the AG the power to come in and make sure we were still in compliance at any time in the future (spoiler alert: they sure would!).

## Failed Retirement: a Painful New Experience

After about five years of essentially the same business day after day, week after week, I had grown a bit tired of it. While it was certainly a profitable venture, it wasn't bringing me much in the way of new challenges, learning, or adventure. I decided to slowly extricate myself from the business by shifting my responsibilities to other people. Once that was done, I first reduced my involvement to part-time, and then largely retired from the day-to-day operations. My plan was to stay home in semi-retirement, remaining only on the Board of Directors.

Rather than taking a final cash dividend when I retired, I had done what I felt was best and left a healthy bank balance of several million dollars to run the company on, just in case they needed the buffer. In the first months after I left, though, the company began to go off track. Sales slowed until they were at break-even point, and then the company started losing money rapidly: sometimes hundreds of thousands of dollars per month! The cash buffer wasn't infinite, and after perhaps a year, they were approaching bankruptcy. There wasn't going to be enough money to make payroll.

I was left with very few options: it seemed as though it were time to padlock the door and go home. Nicole and I considered our options, however, and decided to make another go of it on our own. I terminated the management that I had brought in to replace me, and who had grown the company's payroll but not its sales. That new management had hired aggressively, and the company had bloated with people it could no longer afford to pay, working on projects that simply were not profitable. It needed to be stripped back down to the essentials: software sales and support. In what was one of the hardest moments of my professional career, I also had to terminate about two-thirds of the company staff in a painful all-hands meeting.

If the prospect of being laid off by an autistic software engineer sounds like it would be a cold, impersonal thing, I hope it was not. As discussed in the chapter on empathy, because I've been laid off and terminated from jobs in my own life, this is not a big blind spot for me, and hence, I knew to approach it carefully. Today I know that no matter how many times I've been laid off from jobs in the past, I've never been a middle-aged woman with two children who's been laid off, or a fifty-something-year-old technology worker looking for a new job. There are nuances that I still would have been oblivious to, and yet I dealt with them as best I could. In the end, only those who were there that day will truly know if I handled it well. I hope that I did.

Those we could afford to keep had to start the slow journey back to profitability. It took many months of a slow crawl back to just break even. The intention was to merely stop losing what little was left, and then back to growth so that the company could claim a future of some sort for itself.

## Another Serendipitous Telephone Call

One day in the office as I was tinkering with a sales spreadsheet, the phone rang. I picked up the receiver to be greeted by the president of Support.com, a large, publicly traded Californian company that provided technical support to end-users over the telephone. Ironic as it might sound given my dislike for the phone, we had started to make inroads into the phone support market and had emerged on their radar as something of an upstart competitor. They wanted to talk.

Over the course of the previous six months, I had been able to rebuild the balance sheet and strengthen the software sales such that the business was quite healthy again. Now Support.com wanted to buy it--because we had some expertise in their core area *and* produced a lot of cash from the software side, it would be a great addition to their business structure. They would gain not only new customers but a revenue stream as well. The future was brighter in support, but the money of the day was in software. Publicly traded stocks need both, and this would give them precisely that.

I accepted their offer in principle and we moved into the due diligence phase where the buyer checks the books, reviews the source code to the products, and generally makes sure there are no skeletons in the closet. The only skeleton we had--the attorney general--came roaring out of the closest about midway through this important period in the form of a letter. It was a demand to come in and compliance-audit our business midway through the acquisition's "due diligence" process. If it wasn't a mere coincidence, how they found out about the planned acquisition I do not know. It would be a little bit like getting a dental cleaning during your open-heart surgery.

On the one hand, the AG's request looked terrible because even though we had always complied with the agreement, Support.com had no way of knowing that for sure. From a more optimistic perspective, though, there was no way of knowing for sure until the attorney general had indeed spent its own considerable time and resources essentially doing Support.com's homework for them, in the form of a thorough review of our business.

## A Trifecta of Audits

About part way through the compliance audit, we also received notice of a state income tax audit that would run concurrently. Already faced with the stress of rebuilding a business, combined with due diligence for its acquisition, and a compliance audit, my nerves began to wear thin again. I knew what would happen if I didn't take steps to mitigate the situation, but it seemed there was little, if anything, I could do to improve things. Reality bites sometimes, and all you can do is ride it out.

My solution was to undertake something quite contrary to my autistic nature: I wrote a personal letter -- an emotional appeal -- to Audrey, the assistant attorney general who was the driving force behind the AG's interest in our company. Rather than complain, however, I simply laid out my views on the investigation and the emotional toll it was taking on me. I tried to address each of her concerns as I understood them and to offer examples and assurances that I hoped would at least partially set her mind at ease.

My mindblindness was still a huge obstacle. I had to put myself firmly in her position, with *her* responsibilities and priorities, not my own, and then address each of them satisfactorily. There's really no way to fake that when you're on the spectrum, at least not where I find myself on it. My forthright assurances were well received, I'm told. Up until that point, the AAG had believed I wasn't taking the matter seriously, or that I failed to see it from their perspective. The former had never been true, and now the latter wasn't true either.

Within a couple of weeks, we had completely demonstrated compliance with the AG matter. The extremely thorough nature of that audit combined with its unequivocally good findings served to reassure our corporate suitor that we were the right partner for an acquisition.

## Send in the Marines

All throughout this process, about ten million dollars in cash hung in the balance: if the deal with Support.com went through, it could change our lives. If it failed, it would be a devastating loss, akin to misplacing a winning lottery ticket.

The final piece of the acquisition puzzle was a trip to India to introduce our American buyer to our software partners. It was a company in India headed by my friend Shrishail, who had developed some of our most popular products. I had never flown internationally, and even domestic travel is stressful for me. When I found out that the flight to Jaipur would be followed by a midnight trek through the countryside on a sketchy road known to some as the "Road of Death" to get to the town in question, I began to panic internally. Privately, as much as I wanted to make the trip just for the experience and to visit a good friend there, I absolutely, positively, did not want to go if I could avoid it at this particular time. To not go would look odd, and potentially jeopardize the entire acquisition. And yet I just honestly didn't think I was well enough at that time--what if I did go, and descended into a meltdown in the middle of a negotiation? Could my presence even make things *worse*?

That's when a trusted friend saved the day. Allen was the former US Marine who ran our marketing division. I had recruited him to join me from Microsoft, where we had also worked together, and he offered to go to India in my place. It made perfect sense in almost every way since his was the department most responsible for interaction with our Indian partners anyway, but I was placing a huge responsibility completely in the hands of someone else--which is a difficult thing for me to do at the best of times. He was better at this type of task than I was anyway, but the risks were enormous: I was gambling my future and my retirement on Allen's performance just so that I could avoid a grueling trip to India. That's when you know you're serious about how much you don't like change and don't like travel, and that's when you start to see certain limitations as possibly being part of a significant disorder.

The trip went perfectly, Allen performed brilliantly, and the deal closed a few weeks later. In addition to various bonuses, I accelerated the vesting of employee stock options so that others on the team--Allen in particular--could participate in the sale alongside me. All the remaining employees were being retained (except me, of course), so after saying my goodbyes and taking a last long look around the offices, I handed in my keys, took my check, and went home!

I was still a decade away from an autism diagnosis.

## Back to Coding on the Side

I didn't return to a full-time job anywhere, thus making me officially retired. At first, I headed back to my den to work on computer topics that I had long been interested in but had not been able to touch during my Microsoft career, such as 3D graphics, artificial intelligence, home automation, and so on. Over the years I was able to investigate and build my skills in each, a luxury that only youth or retirement could afford to offer.

Along the way, I would develop other business interests and investments that would prove equally lucrative, but none would ever be so personally fulfilling as writing software. They were work, not play. And so, at the end of the day, that is still what I do with my spare time: I write code. It's not all I do, by any stretch: my kids average about four sports events per week that I attend; I volunteer to teach computers at their school; I'm writing this book; I've built a YouTube channel with 150,000 subscribers ("Dave's Garage"). I take Nicole out frequently and we travel quite a bit. Still, though, I write code every day. By now, I've adapted to the rhythms, if not the nature, of a neurotypical semi-retired suburban life.

While I grant that the opportunity to return to the passions of youth is a rare one, I am surprised at how many of my engineering peers simply have not written a piece of code at all since retiring, not even coding casually or recreationally. Perhaps it's that certain level of immaturity that is often said to accompany autism that enables it, but I am as happy, engaged, and as challenged today as I was riding my bike down to Radio Shack to find computer time as a kid. The field of software development moves so fast that if you're not involved in staying current, it would be easy for my skills to become wildly out of date. Consequently, everything seems new and limitless, and continually fresh. I could do this for a long time . . . and I think I will!

In that way, I'm still that obliviously autistic 13-year-old boy riding my bike to Radio Shack: just not in very many other ways. Perhaps the only affinity I feel for that young version of me lays in that passion for technology. Beyond that, when I look at my young self in my mind's eye, I do not recognize my current self in that image anymore. Is it simply maturity or perhaps has something of my real self been lost in decades of masking?

# Understanding Autism

Autism is not like diabetes, where we have a very good, if not quite complete, understanding of the underlying genetic differences that trigger it. While autism is generally held to be a heritable condition, the genes that influence it are far less well understood. A recent study of five thousand patients identified 61 genes, of which 43 were already known, and many more likely remain to be found.

The reason the spectrum may be so broad, and the characteristics and attributes of the people on it so varied, is that there are so many genes apparently responsible. A child's biological outcome could be determined by whether they inherit one, two, a few, or most of the gene variations that make up the elements of autism. At this point, we simply don't know the precise genetic details. What we do know is that there are enough genetic variables at play that the spectrum is truly continuous, and people can be anywhere on it, and in multiple dimensions.

As we now turn our attention to the actual symptoms of autism, it is important to remember that an autism diagnosis is a complex piece of work performed by a trained neurologist or similarly qualified doctor. Simply having a few (or even many) characteristics in common with people that do have autism does not mean you have a "dash" of autism, because autism spectrum disorder must meet a specific definition.

# Neurodiversity versus Disorder

The "neurodiversity" school of thought holds that people with autism, regardless of its severity, are only different--not less than--and that they do not have a disease or disorder that needs to be treated or cured. In this view, things that differentiate people with autism from the neurotypical give them distinct weaknesses and advantages, but they can succeed when they are properly accommodated and supported.

In the "disorder" school of thought, autism is seen as a biomedical disorder characterized by deficits primarily in communication and social interaction. When someone with autism exhibits an atypical behavior, it is considered a pathological detriment to their social and professional success. Under this paradigm autism is generally something to be treated in order to reduce suffering and to provide the best results for the individuals involved.

For me, autism is best described as simple neurodiversity *up until* it causes unavoidable pathological outcomes. If such outcomes can be mitigated by reasonable accommodations (i.e.: you can adjust the environment to make the situation workable), then that would seem to be the most egalitarian choice. After all, why force people with autism to endure needless discomfort for the convenience of neurotypical people if the issue can be rendered moot with some simple accommodation?

In some cases, however, such accommodation is impossible or impractical. In those cases, if the person with autism can modify their own behavior to accommodate the circumstances, instead of vice versa, it would seem to be a reasonable alternative. To do nothing but suffer--to be a victim of circumstance when not absolutely required--just doesn't make sense to me.

That which cannot be accommodated, nor easily tolerated, rises to the level of disorder. There are many, many times even in my own life where I cannot, try as I might, always "accommodate the circumstances." I believe that's when autism symptoms truly become pathological, and that the condition becomes a disorder: the symptoms cause unavoidable hardship that you would rather avoid but cannot.

I'm also a firm believer in making your own luck, and if undergoing training and therapy to reduce certain autistic behaviors increases your odds of success in the social, dating, and economic/employment arenas, then it's something that I think should be considered. No one should be obligated to do it, of course, but I equate it in this case to having a speech impediment that could be addressed through speech therapy: there is a value in uniformity of speech, just as there is in many other social customs, and thus it makes sense to "go along to get along" to a certain degree. The question of just how *far* one should be expected to go is considered in the chapter Making Friends with Autism.

# Person with Autism vs Autistic Person

There is a great deal of debate in the autism community over language. To me, much of it is confusing, contradictory, and overtly political. The debate over whether someone should be called an autistic person or a person with autism is sometimes heated.

When a topic becomes political, sometimes looking at a simile or metaphor of something less charged can help. To that end, I looked to the simple ice cream cone for a solution. If you are eating an ice cream cone, are you "coned" or a "coned person"? No. You are just a person with an ice cream cone. From that simple bit of logic came my answer. Thus, I would use the phrase "person with autism" over "autistic" in this book. I also decided to generally avoid the use of autistic as a noun, or as a label for a person. My simple rule was to keep everyone a person first, and a symptom second. You would therefore be a "person with the symptoms of autism" rather than "an autistic." I use the word "autistic" sparingly as result.

For a second opinion, I turned to the medical and scientific community, which also uses the person-centric approach of "person with autism."

## Autism Incidence

There is no truly objective way to know just how severe someone's autism is. After some 12 hours of intensive testing by a neurologist, the only numeric quantifier I received was that I am "more impacted" than 98.5% of the general population, and even that was an estimate based in part on subjective measures. Put more simply, there's no simple autism score, or scale, that can be accurately applied to individuals.

According to the Center for Disease Control (CDC) back in 2012, it was thought that one in eighty-eight children was on the spectrum. Two years later, the incidence was revised upwards to one in sixty-eight. If humans did not change that significantly over only two years, and the definitions and criteria had not changed, then the most likely explanation is that we are becoming better at identifying children that are on the spectrum.

What would be more telling -- but that has proven much more elusive -- is a comprehensive study that could identify whether the severity of autism symptoms across society has changed over time. Someone accurately labeled as "moderately autistic" today might have been simply called whatever the then-current vernacular for special needs would have been in decades past. Severe autism might have been mistaken for various forms of cognitive impairment.

More likely still is the possibility that people didn't distinguish amongst forms of neurodiversity or impairment at all, and in generations past, the kinder folks merely said that the girl or boy we now know to have autism was simply "a little different."

Absent more conclusive data, however, it is also possible that the incidence of autism is markedly on the rise, and that we must look for environmental or epigenetic triggers. At this point, we simply do not know.

For our purposes here, however, perhaps the most important thing is that those who do have autism **are properly identified as early as possible**. For those on the neurodiversity side of the debate, early diagnosis provides timely accommodation of any needs that may arise; for those that believe treatment is appropriate, any available interventions that help mitigate those needs can be prescribed.

## Autism Severity

I have largely tried to avoid frequently bracketing autism into categories such as "high-functioning" or "severe."

**Traditional Levels of Autism Spectrum Disorder**

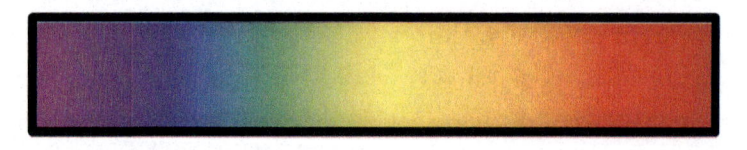

| Level 1 | Level 2 | Level 3 |
|---|---|---|
| "High Functioning" Autism | Autism | "Severe" Autism |
| • Requires accommodations<br>• Difficulties in social situations<br>• Inflexible behaviors<br>• Problems with focus, switching tasks, organization<br>• Obsession with details over big picture | • Requires significant support<br>• Significant social difficulties<br>• Inflexible behaviors<br>• Difficulty or upset coping with stress or change<br>• Repetitive behaviors | • Requires substantial support and assistance<br>• Severe social difficulties<br>• Significant communication difficulties<br>• Extreme difficulties with stress and change<br>• Repetitive behaviors interfere with daily life |

This is not because I do not believe such delineations can ever be made, but because most of the time I don't think they're helpful or relevant to our discussion. For example, if we are examining the notion that people with autism generally prefer to avoid change, this is true across the spectrum in varying degrees. It would add very little information to note that it might be less so with high-functioning autism and more so with severe autism. I leave that assumption to the reader in most cases.

In other cases, however, it does matter; it's unlikely for someone to be both high functioning and non-verbal, so it's accurate to note that only people with more severe autism experience that. For such purposes, then, it makes sense to briefly distinguish between "levels" of autism.

## What does "High Functioning" mean?

All too often I think the "high functioning" label is thrown around the autism community as code for "no learning or cognitive impairments." Used in this way, it sometimes feels like a value judgement. To me, high functioning simply means there are fewer pathological manifestations of one's autism symptoms, and that the person in question can operate, or function, in society with only a few accommodations. It's really a measure of how compatible one is with that society and its social and cultural demands and not a statement about ability or value. It's a measurement of how well you function in your environment – hence the name – and nothing more.

## Where did Asperger's Go?

Most of the psychiatric industry uses a particular book, titled *Diagnostic and Statistical Manual of Mental Disorders, Version 5* (or more commonly, "DSM-V"). In older revisions of the manual, there had been a separate classification for Asperger's, which was close to what most are now calling Level 1 -- High Functioning Autism. At even higher levels of functioning, and with far fewer symptoms, one could previously be diagnosed as Pervasive Developmental Disorder -- Not Otherwise Specified (PDD NOS). At the "lowest" level of functioning, with the most impairment, was Childhood Disintegrative Disorder, which I can only imagine is as catastrophic and tragic as the name implies. It is thankfully quite rare: less than one in one hundred thousand children experience it, wherein a child that was seemingly developing normally begins to regress deep into autism, eventually losing all communication ability. Because this can happen around the age of two or three, the child is often conversant and mature enough to ask what is happening as their world unravels around them.

With its inclusion into the main category of autism, Asperger's no longer exists as a separate condition. According to DSM-V, even "Individuals with a well-established DSM-IV diagnoses of autistic disorder, Asperger's disorder or pervasive developmental disorder not otherwise specified should be given the diagnosis of autism spectrum disorder (ASD)."

Diagnostic criteria aside, the term Asperger's is quite deprecated now due to Hans Asperger's alleged participation in the Nazi's euthanasia program. Time magazine reported that Asperger "participated in Vienna's child killing program. Through his clinic and positions in the Nazi government, Asperger endorsed the transfer of dozens of children to their deaths at Spiegelgrund, Vienna's death center." (Time, 2018)

## Where do I Fit In?

My own diagnosis was "dual" in the sense that it noted I would previously have been classified as Asperger's by older methodologies. Whether that is more accurate than simply saying "I have autism", I do not know. What I am certain of, however, is that those with what is described as "severe" autism face challenges that I can largely only imagine. I do have glimpses of many of those challenges, which lead me to wonder what it would be like if a symptom of mine were two, or five, or ten times worse . . . but I cannot know.

Using the levels chart at the beginning of this section, I'd list myself as "Level 1.5." I am more impacted than the "High functioning" Level 1 column though perhaps less so than the "Level 2" column.

Rather than generalize about the distinctions between the old classifications, let's turn to an actual list of symptoms. As we learn about what defines autism in general, I'll also try to give you a better understanding of my own experience with each of them.

# A Personal Tour of Autism Symptoms

If you are reading this, the chances are excellent that you find yourself in at least one of these three groups:

- Those with a friend or loved one diagnosed with autism spectrum disorder.

- Those with a friend or loved one affected by symptoms that you feel are likely to place them on the autism spectrum.
- Those who believe themselves to be on the autism spectrum based on their own symptoms, diagnosed or otherwise.

I think it's important to reiterate that only an appropriate professional such as a psychologist, psychiatrist, neurologist, or developmental pediatrician should be relied upon for a diagnosis of autism. I believe it's far too important a matter to be left to checklists and surveys and guesses, and the younger the person involved, the more this is true. Early intervention and training are essential in children, and if autism is even suspected, a medical expert should be consulted promptly.

While it stands to reason that the more typical autism symptoms a person exhibits, the higher the likelihood that they are on the spectrum, there is no magic number. Whether someone has an autism spectrum disorder is determined more upon how pathological the symptoms are--how much impact these symptoms have upon the person's daily life, how much social dysfunction, and so on--rather than on how *many* symptoms one has from a list or table.

Certain of the following topics, such as empathy and mindblindness, will be revisited in much more detail later, as they merit more attention than mere inclusion in this list. In many cases we will dedicate an entire chapter to the topic.

> *"As discussions get animated, they hunch forward, prop their elbows on their knees, and start rocking back and forth in their seats, just like Chairman Bill."*

Fortune Magazine, June 18, 1990

## Abnormal or Repetitive Movements

Left to my own devices, I tend to rock in my chair, rubbing the tops of my legs with my hands as I go, while thinking intently about what to do or say next. I saw a lot of this in the computer industry; Bill Gates was famous for it. My best friend does it and was even scolded at Microsoft by his manager for it!

I loved to bounce

Over the years I have caught myself enough times and learned not to do it in mixed company, as it draws attention, but place me in a room with a few good programmers and it seems we'll all be rocking in unison shortly. Why do we rock to deep thoughts? I do not know, but it seems so inextricably tied to autism, and I find it fascinating! Perhaps with autism, as discussed in the chapter on coordination and movement, there is an issue with predictive movement. With a simple bounce or rocking motion, however, momentum carries part of the load and subsequently, the elastic repetition becomes steady, reliable, and accurate. Could bouncing be a way to enjoy predictable rhythms for people that are deficient in creating them? Or perhaps a predictable stimulus of this kind helps insulate one from sensory distractions.

Many children with autism engage in repetitive motions and love to bounce. As a baby, I loved to bounce in what was called a Jolly Jumper, which is a spring-assisted harness, suspended in a doorway. Reportedly I would bounce away without ever tiring of it. Left to my own devices on the school swings, I would wind and rewind the chains to spin me, over and over. Other times I would grab a long push broom and simply spin in circles in the driveway.

## Anxiety and Frustration leading to Depression

I was surprised to find out that anxiety and frustration were symptomatic of autism, because they are the two symptoms that most affect my daily qualify of life, and I had no idea they might be related to it.

Imagine, for a moment, that you are building a house of cards on a polished wooden table in a big, cavernous library. The cards are brand new and slippery--it's very hard to build even a tent let alone a castle. The room is too hot, the tag in your new shirt itches, and you begin to sweat. You focus in as hard as you can, eyes straining until they water, to balance a new row. *You* might find this fun or invigorating--*I* would find it absolutely torturous. But let's continue anyway. You are closing in on that last row when suddenly BANG! -- a child's huge, overinflated latex balloon bursts right behind your head.

The feelings you experience in those seconds immediately following are like mine when trying very hard to do things that are not going well due to frustrating factors beyond my control. I say this to differentiate them from neuroses. I'm not Woody Allen, I'm not scared of the dark. I can be both confident and anxious at the same time, but unless you know me very well, it's easy to mistake that combination for grouchiness or anger. Worse, I can experience this level of anxiety without knowing why.

Aggravated by stress, it can sometimes come on in a wave. For example, I find airline travel quite stressful but still do it. Thus, more than once on the first night of travel out in a restaurant, I've had to excuse myself to the restroom (or even back to my hotel room) lest I burst into tears for a reason I cannot even understand, let alone articulate. At first, I'm terrified for no reason, and next, I'm terrified and sad that I have to put up with that.

## Avoiding the Telephone

I am nearly useless on the phone with my wife for anything more than chit-chat, particularly when one of us is traveling. Oddly, as a teenager, I could spend hours on the phone with girls (with simple idle talk, no doubt), but once I'd fallen in love with Nicole, it became very difficult to have a meaningful phone conversation with her. Quite simply, I must be able to see her face to have any kind of reasonable shot at knowing what she's feeling inside. When alone together in a restaurant I prefer to sit across from her in a booth (or to her side at a small enough table) so as to still see her face. A voice is simply not enough for me, and hence FaceTime video calling has been a great tool.

I do almost everything else by email. I bought my house entirely by email. I buy my cars by email, coordinate their restorations by email, and do almost all my business by email. What I cannot do by email I do online. I earned each of my non-Microsoft incomes online and even had *that* job as the result of an email I sent! What I cannot do online, I do by mail. What can't be left to mail, I plead with Nicole to do for me. When she cannot or will not, I will eventually pick up the phone. And to be fair, I can even be pleasantly conversant on the phone, but it's *hard work*.

One of my favorite friends made a deal with me when we first met. He said, "Dave, if we're ever on the phone, and one of us is just done with being on the phone, let's agree to politely end the call with no explanation needed or hard feelings." And although it's rarely been invoked, this is a wonderful luxury for someone like me. When I first wrote these thoughts in an early draft for this book, I was going to propose that his idea might indicate that he could be somewhere on the spectrum himself, but I suspect now, knowing his conscientiousness, that this was an early accommodation of *my* autism, not an indication of his own!

## Avoidance of Eye Contact or Poor Eye Contact

Eye-tracking problems are common amongst people on the autism spectrum, and I contend with them myself. In my own experience, the avoidance of eye contact in autism feels nothing like the kind you might practice in avoiding a confrontation with a larger, aggressive person. In other words, it's not about social order or dominance, at least for me, though it can perhaps be a mechanism of conflict avoidance -- the way you might look askance on the subway so as not to needlessly invite trouble.

Primarily, though, it's more about communication. In fact, I often *need* eye contact to help me understand the emotions a person is experiencing, as I cannot read emotions from subtle voice cues. For example, if the eyes are the windows to the soul, then reading them is doubly complicated for individuals with autism who have trouble with eye contact. Not only are we operating at a deficit already with respect to understanding the other person's emotions, but we can also entirely miss everything that is communicated by the eyes, which can say so much. At other times when eye contact is not needed to augment the communication, whereas neurotypical people might sustain eye contact as a social nicety, people on the spectrum might allow their gaze to wander toward something else, or even stare at nothing at all. This can appear inattentive to the listener.

If my mood is particularly low, however, I can find it difficult to make eye contact in conversation. This seems to be rooted in a quest for safety--if you represent a danger to me in some manner, I will have trouble making passive eye contact with you. If forced to look you in the eye, I might look aggressive-- probably because I feel threatened somehow. I can look aside, or I can stare, but I cannot fake it and do the friendly dance that one normally does with eye contact. This is probably because the timing is all off. Some experts suggest we follow the 50/70 rule: you make eye contact 50 percent of the time while talking and 70 percent of the time while listening. My eye contact is well-practiced, but I'd never play poker--anyone who knows me well enough could read exactly what I'm doing under duress by the forced cadence of my eye contact.

If I've had a disagreement with Nicole, for example, my own personal version of "tail between the legs" would appear to be "can't look her in the eye."

## Behavioral Disturbances

I'm very emotionally labile: in kindergarten, I would cry when the school band played live; I cry at the end of *Saving Private Ryan* when the old soldier asks his wife for reassurance that he is, in fact, "a good man." And like most men, I'd wager, I cry in *Field of Dreams* when he asks his dad to play catch. But, if it's early in the morning, for some reason, I'll even tear up when an old right guard[*] makes a career-redeeming block in a documentary such as ESPN's *A Football Life*. But if a calamity

---

[*] As but one example, this highlight of right-guard Dan Connoly's kick return is almost guaranteed to make me emotional, and I'm not specifically a fan of either team involved! But why? https://youtu.be/uCa3YMd7f88

like 9/11 occurs, or the alarm sounds in the middle of the night, I'm the rock in the middle of it -- until I process it later, on my own time, in my own way. This attribute of being good at the big things may explain why some with autism are able to function effectively as first responders in stressful situations like being a paramedic. Perhaps low central coherence can be a boon at times: it enables dealing with the immediate situation at hand without worrying about the big picture impact.

Like many individuals with autism, I have experienced meltdowns at times when stress, distress, stimulus, or some combination of them have become too much. Meltdowns are considered at length in a chapter dedicated to the topic.

## Developmental Delays in Language

According to the records my mom dutifully kept when I was a baby, it appears that I learned language normally and today I speak and write reasonably clearly as an adult, consistent with what would have been an Asperger's diagnosis under the older DSM III manual. Those with autism that display more profound social and neurological symptoms often tend to have developmental delays with language, particularly in their early years. Albert Einstein, who is often said to have likely been on the autism spectrum, did not speak until he was three years old. Temple Grandin, a renowned scientist and industrial designer who has been formally diagnosed with autism, did not speak until she was three and a half.

Some have postulated that the delays in speech may result from a difference in the way the autistic brain hears certain sounds, such as hard consonants. In my first years of elementary school,

I did have a consonant speech impediment that was corrected by speech therapy but otherwise learned to speak and read normally. I was moved ahead at grade 3 and labeled as gifted. I have always learned "uniquely" though. For me, there are no such things as subtraction or division, only "opposite addition and multiplication." I do them my own way in my head, not the way we were taught, but it works for me. I am a visual learner and can still, as an example, picture the page of paper that I learned my multiplication tables from as a child. While I enjoyed geometry, I was poor at algebra and worse at calculus. I struggled all through high school, and again in college until I discovered discrete and combinatorial math, which just clicked for me… but the symbol-processing of calculus frustrated me to no end.

And don't even ask me about French -- I was "mercy passed" four years straight. *Je ne parle Français très bien!*

## Fascination with Motion, Particularly Rotary

I realize how this will sound, but from time to time I enjoy watching the washing machine go around. Once or twice I've even propped the washer open and defeated the lid safety switch so I can enjoy the show. I wrote my fascination off as technical curiosity when I recently bought an expensive set of new front-load washers and dryers: yet I watched the cycle to try to determine how it was measuring the load, how the cleaning algorithm worked, what the difference with permanent press was, and so on. After ten minutes of watching the washer, there was more to my interest than technical curiosity, I had to admit. Something about the visual was compelling to me in a way I could not put my finger on.

In the movie *Rain Man*, we find him also watching the washing machine in one scene, ignoring the portable television that his brother has given him. Clearly, the washing machine is more interesting than even television, but why? Our only hint comes when he says that "the red sock falls fastest." He's not merely watching, he's also figuring something out, but to what end?

At the most basic level, participating in such a visual fixation is a form of stimming, wherein people with autism undertake a repetitive, self-stimulating action. Something about the autistic mind seems to derive pleasure from the repetitive, predictable circular motion.

## Fascination with What is Inside

People with the symptoms of autism often seem particularly motivated to learn and know what is inside everything. A clock is seen not merely as a device for telling time, but as a complex system of parts, one that should be understood. I want to know what those parts are, what they look like, and how they interoperate and work. To understand this desire perhaps better, you must know that it is not mere curiosity, but more that it will irritate me *not* to know. It is a drive. *Someone* needs to know, and I feel like it should be me -- in fact, at times it can feel quite stressful not knowing. It feels wrong not to know.

One day years ago, while parked outside my house with my teenaged girlfriend (now wife), we were overlooking some brick pillars that were chained together to form a fence. I remarked that I was curious about what was inside the pillars

-- would they have built them hollow, or with solid brick, or just simple backfill like sand or gravel? How were they constructed? My girlfriend was not only uninterested in the matter but somewhat confused and even annoyed as to why I could possibly care -- of what possible benefit could knowing the answer be? Why would I waste time on such matters? I could not articulate a benefit to knowing, as I had no brick pillars of my own to build, but I still wanted to know and was secretly bothered that she did not. Where was her curiosity? How could this mystery not intrigue her?

We knew then and there that we were very different people, and that it was OK. From then on, I've never lamented our differences and always thought of us as complementary to one another.

As a child I was driven to disassemble everything I could; sometimes, the things I took apart were beyond my ability to properly reassemble, and I got myself into trouble more than a few times. On one occasion, my parents left to do some banking, and when my father returned some ten minutes later to retrieve a forgotten checkbook, he found me on the kitchen floor surrounded by dozens of parts and components from the family stove. He merely shook his head, left, and we never spoke of it again -- but to my credit, I did manage to get the stove back together and working properly before they returned!

## Flat or Monotonous Speech

I must make a concentrated effort when reading aloud, such as giving a speech, for example, to exaggerate the amount of expressiveness and gesticulating beyond the level that would otherwise come naturally to me. I once saw on a doctor's form that I was reported as having a "flat affect." People often just assume that I am grumpy until they get to know me much better. Many, many times I have had people tell me how wrong their first impression of me later turned out to be. We address this topic further in the chapter on masking.

The biggest challenge for me is rapid speech. When trying to communicate a lot of information, particularly to a smart audience, I'm often guilty of what we used to call "high bandwidth communication" at Microsoft -- talk fast, skip the small talk and anything obvious or that can be inferred, just deliver the high points as rapidly as possible. It's a great way for two software engineers to discuss a complicated algorithm, but a terrible way to make new friends at a birthday party!

## Honesty and Codes of Honor

Just as society contains pathological liars, there are also compulsive truth-tellers; they forego socially expedient untruths and kind lies to speak the unvarnished, unpretty truth. And such people are quite often on the autism spectrum. Some with autism are reflexively literal and honest to a fault, and it seems people with autism have a very hard time maintaining a charade of any kind. Sometimes I think those with ASD take the telling of hard truths on as a bit of a showy mantle – as if only they can do it. And while this may be true in certain circumstances, it could be equally true that sometimes discretion is the better part of valor, and hence, certain things are better left unsaid. A youthful person with ASD is often unable to spot the distinction. When my wife tries on an outfit that I don't care for, I don't say it, of course! Yet I can't lie and say that I do, so I'll say something truthful without bite, like "You have a lot of other nice things that might suit today's event better." A complete and literal truth and a bullet dodged!

If those with autism are partly oblivious to the mental state of other people, it is doubly hard to maintain two states--that of reality and that of the lie. We become anxious at the prospect of having to keep track of the lie--or worse, expand on it. Perhaps the most demanding and stressful scenario is for the person with autism to be a party to a lie that they are challenged on, and that they must then fabricate on the fly to support. They are, by nature it seems, poor at it because it is hard to keep track of multiple minds at one time. I could likely memorize a lie well enough to escape detection... until questioned. In practice, I've found that I am largely unable to embellish upon a lie convincingly.

People on the spectrum often operate by internal codes of honor and behavior to maintain consistency, and this is very true of me as well. What we lack in the natural ability to intuit an appropriate response, we compensate for by building internal codes and rulesets that guide our actions almost in an automatic fashion. Operating against them becomes very, very difficult and feels like a serious violation of something: to do so can trigger significant frustration and anxiety. This *doesn't* necessarily mean that people with autism are more honest than neurotypical people, or that they have superior ethics or anything of the kind: it simply means they are often quite poor at the skills of deception.

Coincidence or not, about half of my close friends are US Marines, past and present, and other military branches seem to primarily flesh out the remainder. Perhaps being the type of person who *elects* to live by a set of codes makes for a naturally compatible friend to someone who *must* do so. Perhaps I crave and appreciate a certain logical consistency, or predictability, in someone's behavior.

## Impressionability in Social Situations

All youth are impressionable to some extent; it is, after all, primarily how we all learn how to interact with other humans. We learn in large part by seeing and doing what others do and then doing so ourselves. For those with autism, there is a deficit in knowing how to "act natural." Very little about social interaction feels normal or natural, and so we revert to doing what we have seen others do before us.

Although it predates my ability to remember it with any detail, my mother is quite certain that during my youth, I would "try on" random new behaviors I was exposed to. If I were watching a TV show where the child became sassy to the parent, I would do so too. If I were reading an *Archie* comic in which Reggie is a smartass, I would act like a smartass too. I remember these claims during my youth but thought very little of them at the time, or even during the years hence.

Since my diagnosis, however, I cannot help but wonder if the autistic kid in me was not grasping at straws with respect to how to act. When the social skills, habits, and mannerisms that you need to cope in social situations do not come to you naturally, it makes sense that you will be particularly amenable to emulating others as you absorb how they do it. Watch and learn. Presented with a less-than-desirable role model to follow, I'd still follow along accordingly. Given more positive examples, I would then follow those. I was, in a single word, *impressionable* as I searched for templates to emulate.

Even in conversation today I need to be careful not to pick up the mannerisms, affectations, and especially any accent of the person I am speaking with. What I assume is simply a strategy for adapting and fitting in can be perceived as a mockery if it becomes obvious.

## Lack of Apparent Empathy

As a person with autism, I take a special interest in and occasional offense at this topic. Autism does not (at least at moderate severity levels as far as I can tell) impair the amount of, or the quality of, empathy that a person experiences. It does, however, make it much, much harder for the individual with autism to fully observe, appreciate and understand the depths and intricacies of emotions being experienced by other people. The most important takeaway is that this is a problem of communication and understanding--not of capacity. Once the pain is somehow communicated and then understood, the empathy is as real and as pure as in the neurotypical individual, I believe. The greater complication, however, is how to communicate that state so that the person with autism understands the situation and why it is impactful to the other. To varying degrees, those with autism often lack the ability to read that information from cues that might be obvious to the neurotypical.

An entire chapter on empathy follows later in the book.

## Lack of Coordination and Athletic Ability

Parents of children with autism often report noticing a lack of motor skills before they notice any social deficits; some researchers feel that dyspraxia, or a lack of coordination and motor ability, may be a core deficit of autism, possibly stemming from the same base differences in the nervous system. Approximately 60% of children with autism symptoms will also be described as "clumsy" or "uncoordinated," and I was no exception to the pattern.

Athletic ability and coordination are the focus of their own chapter.

## Lack of Understanding Social Cues

The inability to understand social cues, big and small, is a hallmark of autism. One of the most important adaptations a person with autism can make is to mechanically learn and emulate what seems to come naturally to most neurotypical people: their social graces.

There are many social cues that I am deficient at identifying and processing -- I've tried to improve on these carefully over the years. The biggest challenge for me is in knowing when to jump into a conversation amongst a group. If people simply left a long break or silence in between each person's turn speaking it would be easier, but in an excited discussion where many people are queuing up to get their thought in, where do you jump in such that you are neither interrupting nor missing your chance? And how far afield can you take the discussion with your comment? These are all social issues that can be very confusing to someone with autism. If you want to simulate this problem, at the next cocktail party you attend, wait until the person speaking finishes their third sentence and then-- regardless of where they are in their story -- loudly exclaim, "Did you know that the first Rocketdyne F1 engines had combustion instability issues that almost shook the Saturn V apart?" See what reaction you get. Fear of getting it wrong likely leads to a lot of social anxiety, which in turn makes it even more difficult for a person with autism to get practical experience and practice in social situations.

When I was learning to read in the first grade, the most stressful part of the day was "reading circle", where we would all take turns reading aloud. I could *never* tell when the person before me was done or not. Usually, it would be the end of a paragraph, but not always. Somehow neurotypical humans can communicate the "it's your turn to speak now" indication, but like many other social niceties, it's a cue that is usually lost on me.

## Meltdowns

Most people with significant autism symptoms will experience "meltdowns" from time to time. Put most simply, a meltdown is an intense response to an overwhelming situation; the person with autism temporarily loses emotional or behavioral control. The results can range from withdrawing to yelling, crying, hiding, cursing, or other unexpected and inappropriate responses.

Although superficially they may share some characteristics, a meltdown is not the same as a temper tantrum or panic attack. A meltdown can occur at the same time as a panic attack, though, if enough anxiety is experienced by the person becoming completely overwhelmed.

My own meltdowns have usually been isolated to highly disruptive and stressful events, such as losing one's first serious girlfriend, a major car accident, and so on. There are times, however, where one can become "run down" such that the meltdown threshold is very low, and they become much more frequent.

Meltdowns are detailed further in their own chapter.

## Mindblindness

Mindblindness is the inability to accurately form an awareness of other people's thoughts and emotions. Many believe this is a fundamental aspect of autism. I personally believe I am able to formulate a very accurate picture of their likely *thoughts*, but that I am oblivious to the *feelings*, *emotions*, and *motives* that surround and underpin them. Lacking the ability to intuit the emotions of another, I can only make assumptions. At worst, I will substitute what I would feel if I were you, which is not always helpful.

We also consider mindblindness in its own chapter.

## Not Engaging in Play with Peers

I am not against social play with peers any more than I was as a youth, but for me, such opportunities come second to any opportunity to be productively focused on a project that I am passionate about (i.e., my special interest). In a very real sense, engaging in my special interest may not feel quite like play, but it brings the same sense of grounded psychological satisfaction. Things are good when you are at play, and they are good when you are engaged in your special interest.

At Microsoft, late on Fridays, we would have "Windows Integration Meetings" or WIMs that were large social gatherings in the cafeteria, complete with beer and snacks, intended to make the long overtime nights less onerous. Each Friday I would stop on by. However, once I had spoken with the half dozen people that I truly enjoyed talking to, rather than prolonging the socializing with a beer in hand, I'd seize upon any opportunity to sneak out and return to my office to code!

Sometimes I think kids with autism wind up being excluded from play because, again, they just don't get the social cues of what to do when. If you're little and you spot some kids playing a game of four-square on the playground, there are so many better ways to introduce yourself than to explain to them how they're doing it wrong. But the desire to correct them isn't constrained by an instinct for social norms and out comes the "Hey! You're doing it wrong! Let me show you the right way!"

As noted under Lack of Coordination and Athletic Ability, a general sense of being uncoordinated and generally bad at sports is also very common in autism and serves as a further impediment to athletic play.

## Obsession with Doing Things the 'Right' Way

As just noted, the drive to correct children who were playing a game "incorrectly" was very strong when I was young. I would feel compelled to explain to them how to play the game the right way, a habit that rarely endeared me to the other children. This drive to do things as prescribed does not come from malice or even arrogance: I believe it truly stems from having a rule-based personality honed over years of going along to get along.

This drive might be tempered with age, but it does not go away entirely. Recently I was playing slot machines at the Cosmopolitan casino in Las Vegas, and the person next to me was playing a machine that was fifty dollars per pull. And they were doing it wrong! The person was betting a single credit instead of two credits--a basic requirement for jackpot eligibility--and thus they were not eligible for the jackpot if they were to land on it. He simply didn't know better, not unlike the kids back on the playground. Eventually, I felt compelled to interrupt this total stranger and politely explain what they were doing wrong. Granted, there was an element of altruism in not wanting them to miss the jackpot, but the underlying drive was unmistakable to me: it was the playground all over again.

## Perseveration

Perseveration is the repetition of an action, thought, or utterance, but in this case, I am referring to perseverating thoughts. When a person with autism latches onto a thought that bothers, disturbs, or even impresses them, they can be stuck thinking about it until it is somehow resolved. For things that cannot be resolved, obsessive thinking can take over. They simply cannot let it go naturally. And if they do, it comes back immediately anyway, so it feels like a wasted effort to try.

In my own case, this is complicated because I am a fixer. As a lifelong programmer and debugger, my brain is highly attuned to fixing problems, and if I cannot fix something--such as a loved one's cancer--I must be very careful, lest I perseverate and obsess and worry. Rarely, if this goes on too long, I can work myself into a meltdown.

The more unknowns involved, the worse the worry can be, as each provides a branching-off point from which a new web of worry can be spun--just in case the original wasn't enough!

## Problems with Facial Recognition

Autism can impair the ability to recognize faces, a deficit known as prosopagnosia. Babies who will later exhibit the symptoms of autism appear to lack some of the fundamental social processes that may prompt its development. For example, they often ignore human voices and faces, even of their own mother. Even if the brain circuitry for the identification of faces were wholly intact, perhaps it is simply used less often, and hence the individual with autism is less practiced at spotting the subtle differences amongst faces.

In my own case, facial recognition comes with time and repetition; the more times I've seen the person, the more likely I am to be able to recognize their face. People that I have met once or twice, however--such as an introduction at a cocktail party or meeting a child's friend's parents for the first time--are unlikely to stick. This can cause future embarrassment because on subsequent meetings the neurotypical person will remember meeting me, but I won't remember them. If I have an inkling that this is the case, I tend to own it, and say, "I believe we've met before, but unfortunately I can't place you!" or similar. By the third or fourth introduction, I've usually got it squared away.

I tend to group faces into likeness categories, such that every heavy-set man with brown hair and a beard looks approximately the same. Natalie Portman looks a little like Keira Knightly, and I likely couldn't tell Chris Pratt from Chris Evans. This generally did not become a problem for me until my teen children began to build friendship groups, and I had trouble uniquely identifying and remembering each of their friends, who the parents were, and what they looked like when they came by to pick up their kids. All too often I meet people for the first time who have clearly met me before!

Consider interacting with a Secret Service agent. Behind their sunglasses and muted expression could lie any number of emotions. If they were scowling or laughing or crying, even I could spot it easily. But if they were jealous, or a little suspicious, or hungry or frustrated, most observers have a *much* harder time knowing what the agent is feeling because of the glasses and reserved expression. Reading everyone, even loved ones, is a little like that for me. Ironically, since I pick up fewer of the subtle emotional facial cues, I appreciate the more overt ones even more. I find genuinely expressive people less stressful to be around in some ways because there is less mystery as to what they might be feeling.

Accommodations of and strategies for managing this issue are considered further in the section titled Remembering Your Children's Friends.

## Problems with Social Interaction

I tend to avoid needless social interaction entirely unless it serves some useful purpose -- when I go to parent/teacher night at elementary school, for example, it is to meet the teacher so they can put a name to the face and know that I'm invested in my child's education and so on. It is never for the fun or enjoyment of meeting new people, something I simply cannot relate to. Meeting a particularly fun, interesting, or enjoyable person? Great. But *more* people for the sake of *more* people? No, thanks! It seems most of us with autism do not like large crowds, and that more is not better in social situations. There certainly are gregarious and outgoing people with autism of course... sociability is not a differential diagnosis for ASD!

## Repeating Words or Phrases (Echolalia)

Initially, this was something I thought I didn't do until I started paying attention and caught myself. I do have a few favorite Dad-isms that each of my progeny have heard too many times before, but I imagine most Dads do. Sorry kids, but no matter how many times I say, "I didn't get rich by writing a lot of checks" it doesn't get old to me!

Allow me to give you a simple example: in the movie *Toy Story*, the toy shark imitates the main character Woody by donning his cowboy hat and saying, "Howdy, howdy, howdy!" Since seeing that movie perhaps decades ago, I've used that greeting -- "Howdy, howdy, howdy" -- a million times with my kids.

Perhaps, like Sheldon's door knock* on *Big Bang Theory*, the grouping of three is attractive. I don't say it every time, but I do say it frequently, and I have no idea if it's endearing or annoying to others around me.

It has been postulated that the repetition of words or phrases is how children with autism, faced with a language deficit, attempt to learn. Rather than composing spontaneous complex phrases, they begin by repeating a word or phrase in their head (or aloud) until it feels natural and until that phrase has a home in the brain. Repeating a word can be like scratching an itch in the brain, but one where the itch remains after scratching.

Have you ever written a word, spelled it perfectly, but looked at it and been morally certain that even though you know it's spelled right, it still looks wrong somehow? Sometimes a word feels this way phonetically, in the brain, and repeating the word aloud until it feels natural is the way that someone with autism may attempt to resolve it.

## Resistance to Change

People with autism generally do not like change. At first blush, this might appear to be an attempt to simply avoid the discomfort of adapting to new circumstances, but I believe the reasons are more fundamental: often a change would involve the undoing of a great deal of hard work and thought. Everyone has a certain aversion to change, as it brings on the unknown

---

* Sheldon must knock precisely in groups of three, and any deviation from that causes him significant distress.

and new risks, but people with autism have a disproportionate reaction to it.

Like many kids, I was an incredibly picky eater. I just wasn't afforded the luxury of a second choice at mealtime, so as was the custom at the time, I ate what was provided for me regardless, at least at home. When I was at a friend's house, I would beg off needing to eat anything "strange," generally claiming to be allergic to various things.

My best friend growing up was Chinese Canadian, a child of recent immigrants who still cooked quite authentically. Being the kind of person who cares about the shape and texture of my chicken nuggets, I wasn't keen to try a lot of exotic dim sum opportunities. When dining options were presented, I would continue to claim an allergy to various ingredients. Try as she might, my friend's poor mom seemingly couldn't find anything I wasn't allergic to!

## Sarcasm Impairment

I like to describe myself as a little bit "sarcasm impaired." My first interpretation of what you say will be a literal one. I will then work to deduce what it is that you likely *meant* to say. If what you said contained a significant error or a load of sarcasm, such that the literal and intended meanings are different, sometimes it's hard for me to know immediately which is the case. This is less from an inability to spot the humor than the fact that the sarcasm is often hidden amongst the general inaccuracies and imagery in the way neurotypical people speak. As a person with autism who spots exceptions, I parse the errors and exceptions in almost everything people say. The errors jump out at me, but I overlook the vast majority of them -- along with the occasional piece of sarcasm -- as unimportant.

When my wife and her sisters assemble at a dinner table after supper to chat, they are not highly literal and accurate speakers. Each sister knows what the other ones mean, and by now I also know what they mean, but let's just say it's a dialect. Rather than speaking with precision, they will speak amongst themselves of "that time she said that thing about it to them," usually understanding exactly what the other was referring to. Sometimes, however, as I sit listening to them, only I know that they have a shared misunderstanding, as I'm one of the few translators of this dialect in the world! A few times I have interjected to say, "No, what *she* means is X; what *you* mean is Y," much to their surprise.

It was frustrating to me to have to learn this dialect of casual language use. In fact, it's an ongoing frustration because it serves as a sort of social shorthand from which I am excluded--because I cannot bring myself to get past the torrent of flowery imagery and inaccuracies. Everyone has their own "sarcasm dialect" and it takes a while to learn. Even if the person with autism can process the dialect it will take them a long time to learn to produce it, plus their initial processing will have included some inaccuracies.

I really cannot tolerate the style of banter that some couples engage in, the kind where they jokingly insult each other and lovingly poke fun at each other's foibles. As I take it literally first *no matter how hard I try*, it always stings and is never enjoyable, even if I know the intent is harmless.

## Self-Abusive Behaviors

Only one time in adulthood did I become so intensely frustrated during a disagreement that I did the classic forehead-slapping upon myself -- something that has been observed in people with autism. As soon as the first slap landed on my forehead, I instantly realized how out of sorts I was, how ridiculous it must look, and I stopped immediately. I have never done it again. But I understand how frustration can manifest, and how it must find an outlet.

I don't know if it qualifies as self-abusive, but now when the same intense feeling comes over me -- rare though it may be -- I simply must leave (the room, the floor, the house, whatever). Rather than engaging in any self-abusive behavior, I attempt to flee the situation.

## Sensory Sensitivity

People on the autism spectrum are often highly sensitive to sensory input. The humming of fluorescent lights can be annoying, as can their flicker. The scratching of a neck tag in a T-shirt is nearly unbearable, as is the itchiness after getting a haircut without an immediate shower. If this sounds like the person in these cases is simply being overly sensitive, that's because it's true, exactly that. But the reaction is neither intentional nor elective--they just cannot ignore it.

It is key to remember that the person with autism does not experience the stimulus in the same way that a neurotypical person would. Take the example of the scratchy tag in the neck of a new shirt. When a person with autism puts on such a shirt, it is little different from a neurotypical person doing the same.

In the case of the neurotypical person, however, their brain quickly recognizes the sensation as unimportant and relegates it to the back of the mind, eventually going unnoticed. For the person with autism, however, the brain does not seem to have the ability to selectively ignore certain stimuli. A scratchy shirt tag or itchy wool pants remain so all day long. Those sensations never fade to the background.

When I was a little boy, about four years old, I had to attend my first wedding, which required donning a scratchy wool suit. The pants rubbing on my skin greatly bothered and distracted me, but my mother, to her great credit, made me a little pair of silky liner pants from a smooth material that would buffer me against the scratching. To this day, I cut the tags out of all my clothes, shower immediately after a haircut, and buy only clothes made from smooth, light fabrics.

There are several sounds that I have difficulty with, such as the sound of balloons or Styrofoam cups rubbing on themselves. I do not merely dislike them, however. To me, they are equivalent to fingernails on a chalkboard. I simply cannot tolerate them and must plug my ears or leave.

In fact, it's safe to say that I'm sensitive to and easily disturbed by sound in general. When trying to read or relax at home, I often wear noise-canceling headphones; some people with much more sensitivity even wear them in public as well.

Although I enjoy loud music in small doses, I tire of it quickly at a concert or a club, so I wear earplugs to live performances and remove them only for the songs I really enjoy. When riding with my teenaged son in his truck, I will have to ask him to turn down the music after perhaps one or two songs lest it cause me anxiety. I love to hear what the kids are listening to, but at moderate volumes until I know the song. Novelty combined with intensity is sometimes too much.

As an adult, when we would visit Nicole's parents, Nana would have a steady supply of latex balloons for the kids to inflate, which meant that balloons were randomly popping all throughout the day. I found this random, loud detonation of balloons quite stressful, much more so than anyone merely bothered by loud sounds.

## Sleep Disturbances

Obsessive thinking can complicate my sleep. Sometimes I will awaken in the middle of the night, make a trip to the restroom, and before returning to bed will have revved myself up. Perhaps during the trip, I have had time to reconsider some real or perceived slights from the day, and that could delay sleep.

Parents of children with autism often report great difficulty and irregularity in getting them to sleep. For most of my adult life I have suffered from insomnia, though generally of the initial onset type where it is hard to fall asleep, but then relatively easy to stay there. I have found that the single biggest improvement I have made to my sleep quality is to adopt a regular bedtime and regular wake time, with nap time if needed. Perhaps the times must be largely fixed such that the body starts to follow them naturally.

## Social Withdrawal

My wife and I once attended a gala grand opening for a major new restaurant. Knowing that I'm simply not very good at meeting new people, I resolved that I would change that, then and there. In this city of millions, I was going to introduce myself to the very next person I saw. So, standing at the bar, I turned to my right, extended my hand, and said, "Hello! My name is Dave! How are you?" He looked at me, a little confused, and said "I know, Dave, you bought your car from me this spring!" Which I guess I had... small world! I'm terrible at associating names with faces, in fact remembering faces in general. And I would indeed socially withdraw if not pushed a little (but not too hard, please).

In other words, I try. But socializing absolutely does not come naturally. Not everyone who has the symptoms of autism will also be withdrawn, but I am very introverted, and this seems reasonably common amongst people on the spectrum.

> *Terry:*
> *"Bob, don't you have any other interests?"*
>
> *Bob: "No."*

Pascal Zachary, "Showstopper"

## Special Interests

This is perhaps one of the most telling hallmarks of autism: an intense focus on a very limited set of interests or even one single interest. It has been and remains no less true for me: once I discovered computers, my obsession was armed and unleashed. If not computers, I assume that eventually, it would have been cars or mechanics, or perhaps something else entirely.

The interest itself may (sometimes) change over time, but there is always a burning desire to learn more and know *everything* about some topic. Any hole or gap in the knowledge is like an annoying itch that can only be scratched by learning--it cannot be ignored. In fact, it feels as though only when everything is known, recorded, synthesized, and accessible is the mission complete. Then I'm allowed to rest.

The desire to share and exchange that knowledge, if done at inopportune times, can come across as weird or geeky to the neurotypical. This is where having a friend who is also on the spectrum and who shares that interest can be such a blessing.

Although the topic can drift over the course of a year, for myself it always returns to computers, my first love. Over the course of my life, I have been most interested in technology, but I also restore vintage muscle cars from the 1960s. I know all the Impala and Camaro stats like a classically autistic kid might know all there is to know about the T-Rex.

To give you but two from a thousand trivial examples, I know that the bore of the 1969 Camaro 396 engine cylinder is 4.094" and the stroke is 3.75." I learned *those* nuggets of information when I was sixteen, and I remember where I was standing when I learned them. I also know that the 1969 internal engineering designation within Chevrolet for that engine (one of six offered in the Camaro that year) was the L-34. This means it should have a sticker that reads "JE" on the rear of the valve cover, and it should be equipped with a four-barrel carburetor and an automatic transmission. In the big scheme of my life, details at this level feel roughly as important as knowing that Beijing is the capital of China. Wouldn't you feel at least a *little bit* silly not knowing the capital of China? It's like that. Why wouldn't you *want* to know?

When I was a child, it was the space program. For others it could be baseball statistics, trains, dolls, piano, or poker; the range of potential special interests knows no bounds.

It is common that children with autism will discover their life's passion -- be it computers, math, chess, music, or something else -- early. I've known what I wanted to do with my life for most of my life, and this is not uncommon with autism, though of course not universal, either. Given the amount of angst that so many neurotypical people experience in trying to find their own calling, knowing with great authority what it is that you love to do can be a true blessing.

My own experience is discussed further in the section titled "Obsessive Computer Disorder."

## Stimming

The term stimming is short for "self-stimulating behavior." People with autism often exhibit specific self-stimulatory behaviors, such as hand-flapping, rocking, spinning, whistling, or the repetition of particular words or phrases. In fact, this might be the first thing you notice about a person with autism.

While I do rock in my chair at times, it's something I try to avoid doing very often, at least in public. Likely the biggest stimming behavior I regularly exhibit is snapping my fingers or whistling when I walk.

An entire chapter is dedicated to stimming.

## Synesthesia

Synesthesia refers to the experience of mixed senses--receiving the experience of one sense through the sensation of a different one, like smelling color or seeing touch. To those that do not experience it -- as I do not -- it can be hard to understand. Perhaps the most frequent manifestation of synesthesia is for people to perceive numbers as having color.

Although synesthesia occurs most commonly in the autistic, it is still uncommon even amongst this group. It is rare, but when found, will usually be in a person that also has symptoms of autism.

One of my own sons, who has no other significant autistic symptoms, experiences synesthesia. One day when reading a book, he mentioned that the numbers, although printed in black ink, had colors that he could sense. Curious, I made a private note of the colors he associated with each number so I could repeat the questions later. Although it hardly leads to a scientific conclusion, he reported the same color associations a few weeks hence.

What would be fascinating, but still eludes us, is a better understanding of how synesthesia happens and how it can be taken advantage of. Imagine that the number three was red, and the number two was blue; multiplying them together to get the number 6 might "feel" like the answer should be purple for reasons you can't articulate*.

## Unusual Actions in Public Settings

I knew a fellow in high school named Trevor† who was (I now assume) highly impacted by the symptoms of autism -- he could be loud when quiet was called for, such as in a library. He himself was easily bothered by loud sounds. If he recognized you, he would greet you with an enthusiastic two-handed wave. It's worth pointing out that people with autism who react oddly in a public place are not flouting convention or being intentionally (or even knowingly) disrespectful; they are *oblivious* to what feels normal for others. It makes no intuitive sense to them why certain behaviors should even be normal while others are not.

For those with autism, what often happens is that we become so consumed with the need to express nervous energy or a thought that an outburst must come *now* -- even though we're in the library.

In another example, as noted earlier, people with autism are often very sound sensitive. For example, a high school pep rally, with all its cheering and yelling, might simply be too stimulating to someone with autism. This might cause them to

---

* For me, both the number 5 and the letter E should be yellow. But beyond a few simple associations like that, I don't experience it in any meaningful sense.
† In cases such as this where I could not locate an individual for permission, I have changed their name.

shout out at an inappropriate time or to cover their ears tightly to reduce the amount of sensory input.

## What Next?

Now that we've had an overview of the major features of autism we can turn our attention from the task of identifying autism to the topic of living with it successfully!

# Living with Autism

Now that we have a much better understanding of what the surface of a life with autism looks like we can focus our attention more finely on the most important topics related to living with autism, such as empathy, anger, mindblindness, employment, and relationships.

## Emotions

### Do People with Autism Experience Emotions?

One of the most pervasive myths about autism is that affected individuals lack emotions, or that they somehow lack the ability to understand them. Little could be further from the truth; as we will see when discussing empathy, the problem is one of communication and intuition, not capacity.

People with autism, at least at any level of functioning near my own, keenly experience emotions--usually their own. The deficit lies in their ability to perceive, understand, and intuit the emotions that others are experiencing. They are often oblivious to or misunderstand the emotional state of others, but this should not be mistaken for a lack of concern. Most individuals with autism are more than capable of the love and caring required to genuinely want those close to them to be happy, and like anyone else, it makes us sad to learn when it's not the case. When we do become aware, it pains us in the same way it does a neurotypical individual. We're often just the last to know, or never quite figure it out.

For example, perhaps your cat has recently passed away, and it's still making you a little sad. I can read demeanor and facial expression, so I'll know that you're unhappy, but unless you're really telegraphing an emotion by crying or similar, I won't know what *kind* of unhappy and why. There's even a good chance I will misunderstand your withdrawn and slightly sullen attitude as dissatisfaction or even annoyance with me.

With close friends and loved ones, I've learned to ask outright: Are you OK? What's up? Are we good? With strangers and acquaintances that I don't really know well enough to ask, it can be more challenging.

One significant benefit of the self-awareness that arose following my diagnosis is that now not only am I aware of my inability to read others' emotions, but also, when I do not know the person well enough to pry, I realize that I simply cannot know. And I shouldn't assume anything. I spent most of my life assuming that every cranky tire salesman or blackjack dealer was like that because of something I had triggered, whereas now I can remind myself that they had entire emotional lives going on long before I came along -- and it's probably got nothing to do with me!

## Emotional Post-processing

At the end of the day, or during other quiet moments when I have time to think things over (or to overthink things), I do something I believe may be common amongst people with autism: "emotional post-processing." I replay recent events in my head, and I review the minutiae of my social interactions, most notably of the day that has just passed. I review for subtleties I may have missed, and I essentially grade myself and look for weak spots in my performance. I look for things I wish I *would* have said. I look for things I regret saying and I look for things I should have at least said differently. Sometimes, if things did not go well in some aspect, I'll obsess a little bit (or more than a little bit) about things that turned out to have been the root of a misunderstanding.

I think people with autism also have to post-process their interactions because the amount of social and emotional context that flows from a neurotypical person is simply too much for them to process in real-time--we can easily miss or overlook subtle (and even sometimes less-than-subtle) clues and indications that only become apparent later in retrospect. In this way, I can review the day at my own pace, and this allows me to catch nuances and details that I entirely overlooked the first time. It also allows me the opportunity to scrutinize my own reactions, statements, and behavior, so that I can do better next time. When social and emotional interactions don't come naturally, practice brings continuing improvement.

In some cases, I follow up to try to correct those misunderstandings. Sometimes it's a day later, at other times it's a very long time into the future. One classic example took place years ago when I had a car restored.

*My Pontiac Laurentian, which my Dad bought new in 1969.*

Way back when I was an infant, my Dad bought his very first new car, a 1969 Pontiac Laurentian. A black two-door* with great lines, it was surprisingly cool for a family car, a role it filled lightly on vacations and the odd weekend drive for sixteen years until I reached driving age in 1984. At that point, my parents gave the car to me and like most things that are important to me, I looked after it well and I still have it to this day! I also still have my first football, baseball glove, bat, calculator… and wife!

No car lasts forever, of course, and at over thirty years old it was time for a restoration. Since I was extremely busy with my business, I sought out what I knew to be one of the premier restoration shops in all of America, Musclecar Restorations (MCR) in Chippewa Falls, Wisconsin. I had them undertake what is known as a "complete frame off restoration" where the entire car is disassembled to literally every nut and bolt, each body part is acid-stripped, and every soft component is replaced. Essentially, you pay skilled craftspeople to undertake the painstaking process of hand-building a brand-new, fifty-year-old car, and it took several years to complete.

---

* Because my father had fallen out of the back of that moving vehicle as a child, he would never buy a four-door car for his kids.

Even though this was still in the early 2000s, I managed to convince MCR to do almost everything by email, as I don't like working on the telephone. Nonetheless, there are some things, such as the final inspection, that you really do need to be physically present for, and so when the car was finally ready, I flew out to see the results. With the shop owner and the welders, fabricators, mechanics, and painters standing by in eager anticipation of me reviewing their years of dedicated labor, I silently reviewed the car and absorbed it in great detail, taking numerous photos and notes. I was impressed beyond measure, but my *facial expression* betrayed none of this, and I said very little. When I was done, I genuinely smiled, nodded, thanked them for all their hard work, and told the few I spoke to directly what a great job I thought they had done. Then I paid the final bill and flew back to Seattle.

As the years passed, however, I would occasionally see a glimpse of a television show such as "Overhaulin'" and "Extreme Makeover: Home Edition" where neurotypical people would collapse, faint, scream and cry over restored cars and homes. It's clear that the people on such shows, even if *selected* for their ability to react that way, have created a social expectation for how people are "supposed" to react to such unveilings.

It is most definitely *not* how I react, and it's not how most people with autism seem to react to such stimulus. I believe that I appreciate the craftsmanship perhaps even more and am impressed by the depth of the effort and achievement to the same extent as the next person, but that it does not derail me from normal thinking and processing. I calmly review the situation. Where many neurotypical people seem to lose composure when their name is called to "Come on down!" on "The Price is Right", I'd walk calmly down, nod, thank Bob Barker for having me, play the game, probably win both showcases and forget to smile. We're just different that way!

And so, as I sat in cab of my truck one Saturday morning *ten years later* waiting in the rain for my daughter's soccer game to begin, it occurred to me that I had probably really disappointed the owner and the craftspeople who were expecting a *much* bigger reaction than the one that I had delivered all those years ago. Since I had my laptop with me, I pulled it out and wrote an email to John, the owner of MCR. Because I hadn't been diagnosed yet I still didn't know the reasons why, but I knew that my reaction had not been typical, and I wrote to say that much and to assure him as to just how impressed and moved I had been by the quality of the work they had done. I had said it, I guess, but I had not *shown* it in the way they had become accustomed to seeing from others. I fully expected him to have forgotten about it, but a few minutes later, an email return landed in my mailbox.

It was from John, and it opened with "Dave, I've thought of your reaction *many* times over the last ten years."

He had indeed noticed, and I think been hurt by, the flatness of my response. We wrote back and forth several times until we truly understood each other. Suffice to say, as it often does, my emotional post-processing enabled me to stumble across a problem with my own behavior. I was then able to correct it, to the extent I could, these many years later. Since then, I've continued to have John and MCR work on all my restorations!

In some rare cases such as this, it is possible to go back and set things right. In other cases, it will be impossible, impractical, or inadvisable. Sometimes, as one old bit of wisdom reminds us, it's better to let sleeping dogs lie. Other times it will be worth stirring up a potential source of angst or conflict for the sake of righting it. Only you can know but be certain you are doing the right thing for the *other* person as well and not merely scratching some personal itch at *their* expense.

In summary, most people with autism can understand and experience the entire range of emotions, but their innate ability to intuit the emotional states of others seems compromised. Those with autism often have a deficit in their ability to read and process the emotional cues that are commonly communicated by neurotypical people.

## Empathy

Narrowly defined, empathy is the ability to understand and share the feelings and emotions of another. We know that people with autism can *experience* the full range of emotions, but can they *understand* and *share* the feelings of another person? To really assess empathy in individuals with autism, we must first split empathy into two distinct abilities: the ability to perceive and understand the emotions that another person is experiencing vs the willingness to share in those emotions and to take the appropriate actions.

People with autism sometimes worry that they might be different -- or even defective -- because they know that they process and communicate certain emotions differently than the vast majority of the neurotypical people around them.

Parents of children with autism yearn to believe that deep inside, their child has a full capacity for love and caring. Because empathy seems so inextricably tied to that love and caring, any "defect" -- or even difference in how empathy is experienced or conveyed -- can cause parents to worry that their child does not love or care in the conventional sense. This can be very troubling. *Does my child with autism love me back?*

Those on the outside can tell we are different, and we on the inside know we are different, but how, exactly? What does empathy mean to someone with autism? Does it even exist in people with autism?

Rest assured that, at least from my perspective, the answer is an unequivocal yes.

As leery as I am to even mention psychopaths and autism in the same sentence, we might as well address the topic to illustrate a key difference. I have a friend who believes himself to be on the spectrum and who describes being terrified in his youth with his own worries that he was a psychopath. He came to this conclusion merely because he knew he was wired differently than those around him with respect to emotion. To what extent he was "defective" he didn't know -- only that he was very different.

Is there not some similarity between the two? In fact, no. They're quite opposite both in cause and effect.

As one study put it, "Psychopathic tendencies are associated with difficulties in *resonating* with other people's distress, whereas autism is characterized by difficulties in *knowing* what other people think."

Put more simply, the person with autism *cares* about what you're feeling but often cannot *tell*, whereas the psychopath *knows full well* but usually doesn't *care*. A psychopath can be a master of perceiving the slightest emotional "tell" and exploiting it to their advantage, whereas the person with autism could largely be oblivious to the complex emotional states of others. Psychopaths can be virtuosos of emotion and manipulation, while people with autism are generally the complete opposite.

A person with autism can be fully loving and caring but may at the same time be largely oblivious to what is going on around them emotionally. They can entirely miss the emotional needs of a neurotypical partner or friend. This is a failure of their emotional communication and processing and not necessarily one of capacity or intent.

For me, to understand what another person is feeling I must somehow relate it to an emotion I've experienced in the past. I cannot fabricate and experience new emotions fresh from whole cloth, I can generally only anchor them to my own experiences and assume you feel something like I did when it happened to me. If it never has, I will have trouble.

Perhaps this is true of the neurotypical as well, in that if one has not lost a parent, spouse, or child, one cannot truly know how it feels. Even if that is the case, I believe that the neurotypical are better at intuiting and assuming new emotions in others than those on the spectrum are.

Consider that perhaps someone I know loses their spouse. I would sympathize as much as anyone. But I would struggle to understand the exact emotions and to relate them to losses I had experienced of my own. Since none of my own losses would be directly comparable, my emotional understanding would fall short of that of a regular person. I can and will cry for you but not truly with you, present and in a profound connection because we are *sharing* the emotion together. I will be very sad because it makes me very sad if you are being devastated by a loss, of course! And I will be sad for my own loss of that person. But it is hard for me to intuit how you are feeling when I cannot know precisely what is going on in your mind during those times. It's like when people hear news of a tragedy and say "I can't even imagine" how those involved must feel. I suspect that most people *can*, but don't *want to*, because it is too painful. Whereas I cannot.

But now, at age 50, if you were to lose your father, I can cry with you, for I understand that one from experience. The difference, I believe, is that neurotypical people have an emotional intuition that allows them to know, understand, and co-experience an emotion with another even if they have never experienced that emotion before. I believe it is in part what makes works of fiction compelling to neurotypical readers.

I also realized, only recently, at least one flaw in my own logic above: while I can indeed empathize with you fully over the loss of a father, this is only true if the circumstances are sufficiently like my own loss since it is only through that lens of my *own* loss that I will be able to see and feel and understand yours.

My father and my wife's father were born in the same year and hence were quite close in age. Though they passed away decades apart, each did so quite quickly and unexpectedly from the same disease: stage IV pancreatic cancer. From diagnosis, my dad lasted fewer than 90 days: hers, less than two weeks. Because my father died years earlier it was instructive for me in the sense that I knew that when Nicole's father died that, at least in my own way, I could understand the emotions she would likely be experiencing. And indeed, that largely proved to be true, with one very complicated difference: my father died more than *twenty* years before Nicole lost her father.

Those twenty years make a big difference. I still missed my father, of course, but I was so far removed from the initial shock and tragedy that I forgot what it's like to experience the rawness of it. I had to consciously remind myself at every moment that there are at least five states of grief (denial, anger, bargaining, depression, acceptance) and while I had long since accepted my own father's death, Nicole's own stage in the process over the coming months and even years would be something I would have to consciously remind myself of.

I did not always succeed. More than once, I'm sure, I said things in an attempt to comfort her that only upset her further, and some of it was likely due to my autism. The most common error--and one that I caught and corrected as I could--was to speak of things in a manner that might be absolutely true and appropriate once a death has been accepted but could be perceived as cold in the early days. It could be as simple as pointing out what a great legacy he was leaving behind, perhaps when her pain was still too raw to be soothed by such a weak balm. I remember at least a few times I made the error of attempting to comfort Nicole from my own emotional, logical point of acceptance -- it did not go well; it was too early for acceptance.

The one emotion I did not experience with the death of my own father was one of injustice. He was young (56), I was still young (28), and my mom would be left alone. I could cite any other number of things about his death that were terrible, but I never felt them to be unfair or unjust. My wife, however, carried her father's death more like Inigo Montoya* -- that her father had been wrongly stolen from her, unfairly and unjustly, and it was a wrong that somehow must be corrected. This feeling was so intense a few times that I suspected Nicole even craved a way to avenge her father's death; but she could find no way, of course, because there was no way to be found. As my emotional reaction to my own father's death had not included any sense of wrongdoing, I could not get my head into that space, and so I was not as helpful to Nicole as I could have been. Rather than simply do my best to help her through those feelings, instead, I tried to convince her that experiencing them was somehow *logically* wrong and that she, therefore, *need not do so*. I know from my own experience that this is a terrible way to convince

---

\* A reference to a character in the movie Princess Bride who is on a mission to avenge his father's death. "Hello, my name is Inigo Montoya, you killed my father, prepare to die."

someone of anything and never works -- furthermore, it can be hurtful and annoying.

In both examples, I believe my autism was leading me to assume emotions that I could not understand well enough to mirror -- rather than emotionally experience what Nicole was feeling, the best I could do was to substitute what I thought I *would* (or worse, *should*) be feeling in the same place. Like a shoe salesman running to the back of the store repeatedly to find a pair of shoes that fit, I would do everything I could to find a fit but was ultimately constrained by a smaller inventory of complex emotional experiences in my storeroom.

It's important to stress that this "emotional assumption" is not some act of willful ignorance, it's a lack of ability. To simply guess is literally sometimes the *best we can do when we try our very hardest* to understand what another person is experiencing emotionally. And of course, it varies from person to person.

When the person with autism is very far removed from their element, there are times when it might be better to do nothing, and it is up to the person with autism to learn that fact. When doing nothing is not an option, then it's up to the grace of the people who love the person with autism to not hold them accountable for that which they cannot do well, as long as they're doing their best.

Although not fully understood, it is believed that the brain contains mirror neurons. One way to think of it may be to consider your set of mirror neurons to be a crash test dummy that takes the place of the other person in a debate or debacle. These mirror neurons represent, or serve as a proxy for, the mind of the other person. In your head you talk to -- or argue with, love, or cajole -- this stand-in before addressing the real person in front of you, it's a way of anticipating how they will react. Through these mirror neurons you can also try out and feel the results of what you're going to say or do on yourself; consider it and the mirror neurons will react, and if you're highly attuned to the other person, your mirror neuron stand-in will be a very close approximation of dealing with the other person. All of this happens largely automatically, and you simply sense or "know" what the other person is feeling.

In people with autism, this mirror neuron system is markedly different and does not function as it does in neurotypical people: those with autism must mechanically process what the other person is feeling, with only past experience being the basis of predictions for how their words and reactions will be met. There may be little to none of the internal intuition that the neurotypical seem to have from birth.

In summary, to the individual with autism, it sometimes feels as though the neurotypical individuals have a sixth sense, an almost magical way of automatically intuiting what other people are feeling deep inside. Those with autism, however, must rely on "out of band" information such as facial expressions and explicit explanations. Absent those, and the only hope is to relate the other's experience to a similar one in their own past. Without explicit demonstration that another person is experiencing an emotion, many of us are at a real deficit. Once we identify an emotion is being experienced, some of us struggle to empathize unless we can tie that experience back to something we've lived through in our own lives.

# Mindblindness

Most people with autism have at least some difficulties intuiting the emotional states of other people. It just does not come naturally to them. With mindblindness, however, that inability goes beyond emotions and extends to all areas of the mind.

By one definition, when someone suffers from mindblindness, "the individual is incapable of putting themselves 'into someone else's shoes' and cannot conceptualize, understand or predict the knowledge, thoughts and beliefs, emotions, feelings and desires, behavior, actions, and intentions of another person."

I do not believe, as some do, that mindblindness is a binary state -- unlike pregnancy, which is something you either are or are not. It is clear to me now that the amount a person with autism is affected by mindblindness varies greatly from individual to individual. In my own case, I believe I have a very keen sense of the objective state of the other person's mind -- what they know and what they are thinking. In fact, it is essential for a quick wit -- to make humor generally one must tie the unexpected to what the other person is already thinking. Without knowing what the other person is thinking, this would be very difficult.

Thus, I believe I generally know what a person is likely thinking -- but have almost no idea what they are *feeling about it* without relying on facial expressions or similar.

If, as I claim, I do have an accurate picture of the other person's thinking, though, it begs the question of how I come by that knowledge. What if I am merely smart enough to compute it, using the set of things that I know that the other person knows? I could have profound mindblindness yet still be able to calculate what the other person is thinking with reasonable accuracy. If so, that would seem to reduce my interpersonal skills to nothing more than a clever parlor trick: a keen ability, but one that is a mere stand-in for the natural ability of the neurotypical. Have I simply been faking it all along?

For those of us on the spectrum, much of social interaction is learned slowly and sometimes painfully. I know, based on the rhythm of a conversation, when to nod, when to raise an inquisitive eyebrow, when to smile, and (usually) when an answer is expected of me. But, like an old man getting by with a poor hearing aid battery, I still get it wrong from time to time because I am, after all, guessing. Where do parlor tricks end and genuine connection with another person begin? As we saw with empathy, I believe the problem is again one of communication and not strictly of capacity.

With my autism diagnosis in hand, I began to review most aspects of my life to see where I could identify prototypical autism features, and the more I thought about mindblindness, the more certain I was that I just didn't suffer from it, at least outside the emotional realm. After all, how could I make it through 25 years of successful marriage without even knowing what my wife was thinking... ever?

I slowly realized that I *did* know what my wife was usually thinking. I wasn't oblivious, and I wasn't merely calculating what she was thinking--but I *was* making the fatal error of assuming that she was thinking and feeling precisely what *I would* if I were in her position. And therein lies the trick to it: I can indeed put myself into other people's shoes, but I do so more literally than most others. I see their perspective through my own eyes as if I were in their position rather than through theirs. While that often works, as you can imagine, it also often fails or leads me to erroneous conclusions, particularly about intent. The old saying goes that one should "never attribute to malice that which can be sufficiently explained by [X]", but when you can't think of a non-malicious explanation because your understanding of the other person's mind is contrived, limited, or worse -- absent -- a person with autism can assume malice by default. This leads to a lot of conflict if not caught.

As a trivial example, I recently upgraded my internet service, but while the billing change took immediate effect, the speed increase did not. I called their technical support department, and in speaking to one of their representatives, I made several bad assumptions. When the problem looked to be more complicated than originally thought, and it seemed to me as though the tech was just trying to get me off the line, he said that I would need a "new account application" and to contact a sales representative. Having been a customer for some twenty years, I was offended at being treated like a new customer and frustrated by his apparent attempt to punt me to another department. I became annoyed and my tone changed noticeably, complicating the conversation needlessly.

This was entirely an error on my part. The "account application" was not to apply for a new account. He meant I needed to run a *computer application* to finish the upgrade that the sales department had not. He was attempting to be helpful but based on poor experiences with that company's support in the past, I presumed he was merely trying to get rid of me. My limited context--not to mention my poor communication ability over the telephone--combined with a language barrier to give me an incomplete set of facts that I used to build an incomplete image of the representative in my mind--and worse, I trusted this interpretation to be accurate without questioning it.

You might look at this example and think it could happen to anyone -- and it could. If you have autism, however, it happens *all the time* in your interactions with other people, including loved ones, and not just over the phone. Worse, it happens in scenarios where the neurotypical person believes that you know how and what they are feeling while the person with autism simply has no idea.

If you've ever argued with someone who is being willfully ignorant, you know how frustrating it can be. Sometimes I imagine that it might be similar for a neurotypical person dealing with someone that has autism: we might appear as though we are being obstinate, refusing to "get it", when try as we might, we simply cannot. It's not that we do not want to! At least twice I have sat in (friendly) marriage counseling sessions where my wife and the counselor exchanged glances that clearly told me I had totally missed something important, and yet I had no idea what. So, I've had to interrupt and say, "I know you may not believe me, but I am *totally* oblivious to whatever you guys are thinking right now." They had to explain to me.

Since my diagnosis, one of the hardest things to convince loved ones of -- perhaps because I've faked or hidden it so well until now -- is that I cannot read emotions unless I can see your face. The worst is if someone I'm in a heated discussion with simply turns and walks away -- even if they are still talking. Without the benefit of being able to see their facial expressions, I will often have no idea whether their closing remark was in earnest or sarcastic, for example. I will then assume either one or the other, locking in that perception until our next in-person interaction. In a very real sense, I snapshot the last known state of another's mind and hold onto it as a proxy for the real person. And that mental proxy is quite often a very inaccurate picture -- but it's all I have to go on.

If one's theory of mind is that it consists of the ability to both construct and maintain a mental proxy for the other person, then I argue that in autism it is primarily the *construction* aspect that is impaired: once the state of the other person is satisfactorily communicated, a person with autism might be able to hold it and maintain it. But they cannot get there on their own.

Perhaps in cases of more profound autism the individual truly is completely oblivious to the emotions, feelings, and thoughts of others, but I believe in most cases the solution can be found in better communication. This is particularly important in a marriage where one of the partners is on the spectrum.

# Monofocus, Hyperfocus and Bracketing

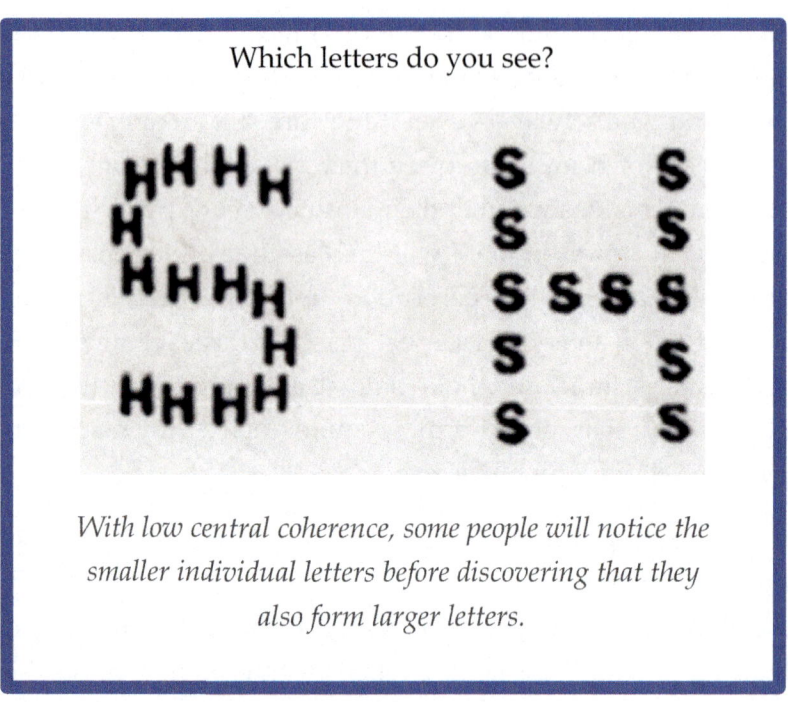

> Which letters do you see?
>
> ```
> HH H H              S           S
> H                   S           S
> HHHH                SSSS
>      H              S           S
> HH HH               S           S
> ```
>
> *With low central coherence, some people will notice the smaller individual letters before discovering that they also form larger letters.*

Dr. Temple Grandin, TED Talk
Reproduced with Permission

People with autism often lack strong central coherence, which is to say they tend to focus on the details of something rather than the big picture. Even if everything in their life is going quite well, when one important aspect of their life is not satisfactory, they might very well dedicate all their attention to that -- to the exclusion of other matters.

While I prefer the term monofocus, much has been written about central coherence and monotropism as it relates to autism. A monotropic mind tends to focus on the details and miss things outside the attention tunnel. Within the attention tunnel, however, deep thinking, intense experiences, and altered flow states are possible. A state of "hyperfocus" is often possible for some individuals.

These attention issues would seem to fall under the banner of attention deficit disorder (ADD) and indeed, ADD is a common feature of autism, and so these symptoms are probably not entirely separable from it. If you have the ADD features, it ultimately is of little import whether they are part of the autism disorder or if they are separate entirely: what matters is whether you are aware of them and how you manage them.

"Bracketing" is the term I use for the way in which my own brain cognitively sorts people. At its most basic level, my brain will bracket and organize those around me into broad categories, such as friend, helper, academic nemesis, danger, dependent, or whatever *primary* aspect of our relationship is important at this moment. The very same person might be bracketed completely differently hours or even minutes later, based on a shift in perception that changes who they are to me. My family members are always in the "loved" and "trusted" and "must protect" buckets, but they might also be categorized as adversarial to me in some contexts such as a game of Monopoly.

At one end of the social spectrum are the salespeople and politicians, the Bill Clintons of the world who have mastered the ability to remember everything and anything important about every constituent they've met in the last 20 years. At the other end are people such as me, who necessarily bracket people into broad categories such as "this guy knows carpentry." Try as I might for many years, I am simply unable to remember the tiny details of "This is Michael, he works at Sears with your cousin Maybell, and had short hair at last summer's reunion." After hearing such a sentence, I guess there was a reunion, I think it was last summer, and I now know that someone works at Sears, and someone has short hair (the details) but not who the person is or why it matters to me (the big picture). I come away from that with a cup full of puzzle pieces, not a complete picture.

I do not create a complex mental identity that I track and associate with each person. Rather, for most simple acquaintances, I'll remember very little beyond the raw utilitarian -- perhaps what they do and what they know. If you're the captain of a cruise ship, or you know how to tie a double Windsor knot, those are the things I remember about you most. You might, then, find it odd if a year or two later I think of Cathy's husband strictly as "That shorter guy with the big knot to take up the extra tie length." That's how I remember people though, by what they know how to do.

It's almost as if I've built a repertoire of who knows what in case I have a need myself: a purely *functional*, rather than *social*, memory of who is who.

## Monotropism and Problem Solving

If a monotropic thought style truly limited one's mind to thinking only of one thing at a time, it would render people with autism into rather poor general problem solvers. After all, arriving at a solution quickly might require innovative thinking across a wide range of concepts, and if one's mind is too rigidly fixed to a subject, how would one ever arrive at an innovative, off-the-path solution?

This is because monotropism is not a limitation of subject matter, but rather a super-heightened sense of priority for a particular problem or topic. As an example, being a person with autism, if I am having a disagreement with a cashier over how much change I received, I might focus unduly on solving that problem while ignoring others. I might not notice that people are queuing up behind me, waiting in line. I might overlook the trivial cash value of the coinage in the quest to get the number correct. The immediate problem at hand -- getting the correct change -- takes on a much higher than normal priority and other issues are pushed to the periphery or ignored entirely.

This approach to problem-solving -- making the problem at least temporarily the most important thing in the universe -- is a handy tool for software and engineering, perhaps, but can at times be cumbersome in personal relationships.

## Arguing with Autism

People with autism can be difficult to deal with when they are agitated or angry because they may not respond in the same manner as neurotypical people might when confronted with the stresses of an unwanted situation.

Monotropic thinking focuses all one's attention and top priority upon a singular problem. While this may make for robust problem-solving skills in the engineering domains, it can make someone with autism not only a formidable arguer but also maddeningly frustrating to deal with at times.

When you combine that monotropic thought process with poor central coherence (being able to always keep the big picture in mind), a person with autism can easily become completely consumed in an argument and even descend into a meltdown if the subject matter is sufficiently important to them. At some point in the argument, a neurotypical individual will no doubt experience the notion that the person with autism seems to be taking the matter *much* more seriously than they do, indeed, more seriously than seems reasonable for the subject at hand. And furthermore, their reactions and emotions may be so accelerated that they become visibly upset, crying, or yelling in a situation that would not normally call for it.

And yet, from the perspective of that individual with autism, it is by no means an overreaction. If anything, they will be confounded by the notion that others do not take the matter as seriously as they do, and this realization may even escalate their emotions further. A certain panic may set in that "only I get it" and the others around not only fail to understand, but they'll also probably repeat the mistakes that led us here in the first place.

Clearly, I can speak with greater accuracy about my own autistic thought process than I can about others, so allow me to formulate a hypothetical example that would be typical for me.

Let us say that I am confronted with "problem X." X is not a matter of life and death, let's say, but it's a serious issue -- an illness, a major relationship upset, or something of that level. My first reaction upon learning of X will be frustration, simply because the reality is far different than what I would like to be the case. If it's an issue that someone has caused, whatever has happened was likely avoidable if they had only gone about the thing the way I would have preferred, at least in my mind. This frustration will often be read as anger by those around me, but it is wholly different. Frustration may *lead* to anger eventually, but it is not the same thing. Now, most likely, my friends and family have *two* problems: X and my own reaction to X. There is an echo of this in one popular episode of *The Big Bang Theory* where the character Sheldon has his apartment broken into and burglarized. The conflict at the core of the episode stems from attempting to manage Sheldon's reactions to the burglary, not the burglary itself.

By now I can tell when loved ones start to worry about me and my reaction. That very recognition can raise emotions that compound whatever problem X was to begin with. I experience not only shame and regret from knowing that my reactions might be over the top and inconvenient for those around me, but simultaneous resentment that the matter isn't seen with equal seriousness as it appears to me.

The problem from this point forward is *how* serious the matter feels to me. Because my mind can only entertain thinking about one high-priority issue at a time, my worry over X expands to become all-consuming, commanding all my attention and intellect until I solve it. And because I lack strong central coherence, I almost always overestimate how serious the matter is relative to everything else under the sun. It will feel essential to avoid an unacceptable future where problem X recurs. It always feels as though, absent a solution that everyone is on board with, I have entered a world with a "new normal" that I am unable or unwilling to accept.

If I believe that I know the solution to the problem but that it requires others to cooperate or implement the solution, I worry a great deal about whether others will take it as seriously as I do. In some circumstances, I believe I have subconsciously acted out or escalated my rhetoric (or even profanity) simply to provoke participation or discussion where I felt it was being overlooked, not because I wanted attention upon myself, but to direct adequate attention on problem X. In this way, my behavior was acting as a forcing function to focus people on the problem. This is not a good tactic.

This issue of recurrence is paramount. I am not overly concerned with apologies or explanations, nor retribution or anything rearward-looking. All I really care about at that moment is avoiding the same problem in the future, and that requires two things: (a) that everyone understands the solution, and (b) that those involved will make their best effort to avoid a repeat. In the few instances that both have happened very early in a moment of upset, such reassurance can almost entirely dispel the anxiety.

A popular Korean/American television series titled *The Good Doctor* features an episode wherein the character with autism, Dr. Murphy, is experiencing great stress over learning to drive. At first, he obsesses over the belief that he is being railroaded into learning to drive against his wishes. As he believes (rightly or wrongly) that he lacks some innate ability required to do it safely, he "knows" he will therefore undoubtedly perish in a horrible accident. Worse, it will have been a predictable and wholly avoidable fate if only people had listened to his very real concerns. His entire world collapses to a singularity and everything else becomes incidental -- at that moment, all that matters in the universe is that he is not forced to drive again. He's so consumed with that one thought that he's as oblivious to the dangerous traffic zooming by right now, as he is to every other priority in his life. There is one thing in his mind -- the belief that he will perish against his will in some future car accident and that he must prevent it here and now.

At this moment his companion -- whether by design or by accident -- does something nearly miraculous and ends his ensuing meltdown in the early seconds. She tells him adamantly and repeatedly that he does *not* need to continue to learn to drive. He can abandon the effort entirely if needed. The choice is *his* entirely and *he* is in control of his destiny.

She also needlessly capitulates and accepts the blame for having forced him to drive in the first place. In the context of this TV episode, it might have been both true and relevant, but I would not normally advise taking the blame in such a situation. I don't believe that humoring someone with autism is dignified to begin with, preferring the literal truth. Having a scapegoat does me little good as I'm much more concerned with future recurrence than with assigning blame for the past. I would also no doubt see through such an attempt and ultimately lose confidence in the person's sincerity, and therefore, effectiveness in solving future dilemmas. Simply saying anything to de-escalate a dispute will soon be seen as ineffectual, and likely would not work for long anyway.

Her reassurances to Dr. Murphy are specific, true, under his control, and resolve the problem entirely. It does not mean that he will never drive again--it only means that he controls the choice. Other times a literal truth will suffice: if a teen is panicking in the summer about heading off to college, perhaps knowing that in theory they *could* bail and return home after three or six months resolves the issue sufficiently for them.

Imagine a much simpler problem -- a child is being taken to a favorite restaurant that serves his one and only favorite chicken tender. When they arrive, however, it turns out that they are all out of his chicken, and the child is despondent and unwilling to eat anything else. A meltdown seems unavoidable. Even doing nothing is not an option, and will have the same result, so what to do?

If I understand the autistic mind at all, I'd wager that there are two dimensions to the child's upset: first, the immediate and visceral loss of the opportunity to have their favorite thing right now, and second, the intense frustration from the unacceptable reality of living in a world where this is the new way of things -- the child will always be forced to eat things they hate, and this was probably avoidable. After all, if it can happen this time, it can and likely will happen in the future if we keep doing things the same way.

The first part, the lost opportunity, can't always be fixed, notwithstanding the miraculous heroics that I'm certain some parents have undergone in circumstances just like this! But sometimes a resolution of the second part can bring enough control and optimism to steady the ship. How, then, to accomplish it? Of course, it entirely varies with the intellectual ability and maturity level of the child in question, not to mention their own unique personality, but my practical suggestions would be:

- Assure the child that you will talk to the kitchen and determine the actual brand details (so that you can locate other restaurants that might serve the same going forward).
- You'll tell the chef or manager how much you like them and ask them to please continue to order/use the same ones for as long as possible.
- Resolve to phone ahead next time, so that there is no surprise about availability upon arriving.
- Next time they are available, place a second order to take home and freeze for emergencies. They're not as good that way, perhaps, but they're the "same," and sometimes that's even more important.

Any tactic that reassures your child about the future is good -- even if it does nothing to help the immediate "now." That sting has already stung, and only the future matters.

Even if such assurances do not bring immediate resolution, they will likely go a long way toward stopping the inward rumination that might otherwise end up in a meltdown. The assurance goes to the core of the obsessive thought patterns that might be internally escalating. There might still be upset, but hopefully, its duration and intensity can be limited.

# Bullying and Teasing

In a recent survey, more than 90 percent of mothers of children with ASD reported that their child had been the target of bullying during the previous year. Being bullied can lead to low self-esteem, anxiety, depression, social isolation, and poor school performance. The effects of being bullied can last a long time -- decades, if not a lifetime. Such bullying can be a major contributor to depression, anxiety, and anger management issues in adulthood.

Like most kids on the spectrum, I was bullied extensively as a child. Like many children who are so tormented, it was formative in the development of my personality and outlook. And yet one of the most cathartic episodes in my life took place the night after receiving my original job offer from Microsoft in 1993.

That night, I had a dream in which I revisited many of the bullies that had assaulted me, and in the dream, I righted those wrongs. In most cases, merely returning to confront and intimidate the bully was sufficient, but in one or two, I dreamt of revenge. But in each case, I obtained closure, and upon waking in the morning, felt fresh, as though much of the childhood torment simply no longer mattered. It was like years of therapy in one night -- with one exception: Joey Roberts.

Joey Roberts was a small, red-haired stepchild of a kid that probably took more beatings than he ever doled out, but one day, he punched me in the face for fun. Literally.

Way back in sixth grade gym class one morning, I was sitting on a bench up against the wall and Joey walked up, and with no explanation, punched me full and directly in the face, as hard as he could. With only the strength of a kid, no teeth or bones were broken, thankfully. But suffice to say, I was stunned, but largely did not react. When later confronted by the school authorities, he explained plainly that he "always wondered what it'd be like to actually punch someone right in the face, and who'd care if I punched Plummer?" It was that last part that really stung. And I held onto that resentment and bitterness for decades. His was the one bit of bullying that I just couldn't let go of.

One day, just a few years ago, I was visiting my brother back in Saskatchewan. We were at Home Depot looking for a part to complete a project he was working on, and when I rounded one corner, I almost ran full into a worker whose hair color nearly matched that of his orange vest: it was Joey Roberts, in the flesh.

Joey is about 5' 2" and maybe a hundred and fifty pounds. I am well over six foot two and a solid two hundred pounds[*], so I effectively towered over him. By accidentally surprising him as I rounded the corner, we were only inches apart, face to face.

Despite the decades, he knew immediately who I was, and a look washed over his face that seemed a combination of contrition, embarrassment, and sadness -- then fear: I may not be good at reading many things, but obvious facial expressions I can manage. I could tell that he'd been carrying a load from

---

[*] About 1.88m and 91kg

that incident for all these years as well -- but a different one. The remorse and guilt on his face were all I needed to see. Though in truth I thought of it very rarely, it was the one incident I could never let go of, and it vanished in a flash with just a look. I put on my best mask complete with a friendly smile -- this time genuine -- and shook his hand as though we had last parted best friends.

## Acting Different

While it is certainly true that bullies typically pick on children they perceive as weak, it is also true that there is a wide selection of weak children to choose from, so what is it about children with autism that tends to attract their wrath?

One key factor is that children with autism tend not to roam in packs! For example, a child with autism may be able to tolerate the stress and required masking of the classroom for a few hours but might need the respite of recess to take a break and be away from other people for a bit. This alone time exposes them to greater risk. But is there anything about the behavior of the child with autism that attracts bullying?

I must tread carefully here lest I wander into victim-blaming, which I would never wish to do. It should go without saying that there is *no* amount of acting differently that would merit or justify the attack of a bully. I do not mean to imply any such thing, but it remains clear that bullies prefer kids with autism as their targets, so unless and until the adults create an environment that is somehow fully protective of these children, it makes sense for them to act in a manner that attracts the least punishment. Which is to say exactly like the neurotypical kids. But what is the difference?

The difference would appear to be *any* difference. I believe humans in general, and kids in particular, are xenophobic by nature and that it should (indeed, must) be trained out of them to make them functional members of a diverse, global culture. Since that is not happening fast enough, or perhaps at all in some cases, bullies remain in our midst. These bullies target kids who act differently in part because doing so seemingly signals weakness. Different equals alone, and alone equals weak.

I did not have many overtly autistic behaviors when I was a child; I did not yelp or flap my hands when stressed. But even being a child who simply matures a few years behind his peers, and who finds different things funny than they would, is apparently fair game. It's likely that my bobbing, bouncy, uncool gait was an early signal of being a target as well, and so I can only imagine the difficulties faced by children with autism that attract even more unwanted attention.

If acting different invites punishment, and if -- as I've asserted elsewhere -- people with autism naturally try to emulate and adopt the social behaviors of their successful peers, why then do not kids with autism simply learn to act normally? (Which again, is not to imply a duty or obligation to do so.)

I believe the reasons are multiple. First, because kids with autism tend to mature more slowly than the kids around them, even if they appreciate the behavior of a more mature kid, they might not yet be equipped or able to undertake it on their own.

Second, they might be physically unable: perhaps the local kids are all learning the yoyo or perhaps exchanging a cool, new, secret handshake -- the kid with autism would love to learn also and be part of the crowd, but he lacks the fine motor coordination of his same-aged peers. As a result, his desire to emulate the other kids and to fit in cannot be satisfied. Third, it might simply conflict with the way the child with autism is and the behaviors that they either wish to exhibit or that they cannot contain. If hand flapping is not cool, and you must flap your hands when excited, then coolness will be elusive amongst that group.

Kids with autism that are less mature than their peers may exhibit behavior that is considered intrusive, irritating, and provocative by neurotypical kids. They may not know how to read the social situation in which they find themselves. This leads to perhaps inappropriate actions and reactions; the child with autism may not know how to participate "properly" and hence will act in a way that attracts unwanted negative attention from their peers. Further, children on the spectrum can have difficulties with the process of characterization, which is essentially sorting people into "good" and "bad." As a result, kids with autism may lag in their ability to properly identify those who can be trusted and those who should be avoided because they will only bring them misery.

Somehow, a balance must be struck between individuality and "going along to get along." In a perfect world, all children would be accepting of one another's differences and embrace those differences, but that is not the world we find ourselves in. While our schools and society at large can -- and must -- make efforts to protect children who act differently because of their autism, social training that reduces the amount by which a child with autism stands out can help reduce the amount of unwanted attention the child receives.

One of the most frustrating parts of being a youth who is being bullied for being different is that they rarely tell you specifically what everyone else already knows, and that is *how* you are acting different and *why* you are being bullied. It is akin to a blind person being bullied for their lack of sight: people with autism are often bullied for being *socially* blind. Lending guidance to a youth whose behaviors and mannerisms are attracting the unfortunate attention of bullies might, philosophically, feel entirely wrong because we're asking the *victim* to change. And philosophically, of course, it is entirely wrong to ask the victim to bear the cost of mitigating future attacks. From a practical standpoint, however, some whack-a-moles get tired of being whacked and would rather know when it's best to keep their heads down. Equipping the individual with autism with the tools to successfully navigate a sometimes-cruel world is never wrong.

## Coordination and Movement

If people with autism can be said to think differently, it is less well known but perhaps equally true to say that they move differently as well. The DSM-V psychiatric handbook used by most American doctors does not include movement irregularities as a diagnostic criterion for autism, only as a typical characteristic, but other classification systems around the world have listed it as diagnostic. Either way, suffice to say there is a strong connection between autism and problems with movement and coordination. Children with autism will often be late to reach developmental milestones related to movement such as sitting, crawling, and walking. Approximately sixty percent of children with even mild autism will have their movements described as "clumsy" and "uncoordinated." The clinical name is dyspraxia.

Exceptions abound -- but I was not among them. My basic developmental milestones were on time, but by the age of five, my athletic and coordination problems were apparent even to me. My dad played "roll and catch" with me regularly and dutifully took me to T-Ball* events and similar, so it was not for lack of opportunity.

As an example, at age eight, I was so bad at baseball that I could only make the local "sandlot" team where *no one* gets cut and your uniform is a T-shirt bearing your number drawn on with a black Sharpie. To do even that, Dad had to agree to volunteer to coach the team. And he only let me play left field, and only for three innings per game, and that *was* being generous! I can firmly recall the shouts of "Move up!" from other teams when I came up to bat, though whether I ever actually hit the ball, I cannot recall. I did get on base once somehow (perhaps walked or beaned) and when the next kid hit the ball, I was slow enough that he had caught up to me by third base! This experience was to be repeated across almost every sport I would attempt to play. I was always strong for my age but

---

* A version of baseball intended for small children where the ball is served from a tee rather than pitched.

woefully uncoordinated, and to this day I have literally *never* worn a sports uniform.

As I imagine they can be for a lot of kids with autism, my physical education classes, such as gym, rope-climbing, track and field, etc., were also a bit of an ordeal. Striking out and failing at something as simple as the game of kickball brings a great deal of embarrassment, and many kids who find themselves in this predicament will simply begin to shy away from sports. Presumably, they wonder why they would put up with the torment and failure if it can be avoided? Hence the very kids who need the *most* repetition and practice will inevitably get the least as they understandably avoid competitive sports -- even developing convenient maladies that allow them to miss their physical education classes at school.

Fundamentally, I believe kids growing up with autism face challenges in coordinating their *intent* with their bodies, which manifests not only in sports but also in any area requiring fine motor control, such as handwriting. It is as if the child knows what should be done, but the hands, feet, and body are not willing or able to follow along quite precisely enough. Imagine learning a new dance where you know intellectually what to do but the body does not yet comply. It is similar with a sport as simple in theory as bowling or golf: you know exactly where you want the ball to go, and hence what you need your body to do but, particularly if you are new to the sport, the body cannot follow your desire quite precisely enough to achieve it. The problem with autism is that this level of uncertainty and intentional effort applies not only to new dances but to things as seemingly simple as sprinting or hitting a ball ... and even walking.

According to a study of brain imaging, children that have autism must rely much more on conscious planning, activating the brain regions involved with such, and less on the cerebellum, which automates movements. If our movements never become routine, they also never become natural and fluid. I cannot, however, rationalize this with the fine motor control obviously necessary for playing a musical instrument such as the piano or saxophone. Since many people with autism have excellent musical ability, clearly not everyone with autism is impacted equally.

As a young teen, I remember friends trying to get me to "walk more like a cool person." Try as I might to emulate the gait of my peers, I could not achieve the pure, lackadaisical, unintentional efficiency that they had. If you're watching *Cool Hand Luke* and Paul Newman saunters into the frame, he uses the minimal amount of energy required. He's not in a rush and his movements are fluid, each one a simple precursor to setting up the next. That's cool -- and it can be very hard to reproduce for someone with autism.

I can still remember having difficulty learning to tie my shoes, in that I knew how to do it, and I could visualize and understand how the loops went through one another, but I could not get my hands to comply and follow along in the right order as I wanted. I do not know for sure, but I suspect a neurotypical kid learns this differently: by simply going through the motions until the muscle memory has made the effort seem natural. With autism, it's possible that the movements never feel natural, or that they take much longer to do so and always retain a deliberate feel. At least initially, the movements must be planned and painstakingly executed in a very intentional fashion. If you try to think through all the individual steps to tying your shoelace, the very act of doing so might cause you to make mistakes. Of course, even with autism, sufficient repetition can still breed success and within a few days, I had mastered the tie. But it did not come as easy as it might have for other kids.

Even today, at the gym, if my trainer has me get into a position to stretch, and then tells me to reverse it, it can take me some time to mentally turn the position around. The mirror only complicates matters: often, I will have to ask for specifics. Even though my 3D visualization ability is excellent when visualizing or manipulating other objects, putting my own body into a particular position after seeing someone else demonstrate it is always challenging, and "reversing" it is even more so. This is particularly true, it seems, for any cross-body movement.

When the autism symptoms are minor and the impact on motor movement is subtle, I would imagine that unless a child's mother (or another primary caregiver) has a great deal of prior experience such cues are easy to miss; whether the child takes an extra month or two to walk may not be material. It might only be in the context of a larger group of children that the differences come into the light. Perhaps kindergarten and PE teachers become adept at spotting the somewhat characteristic movements and gait of kids with autism, even if they are unaware of how such movement corresponds to the condition.

On the bright side, although there were to be no sports scholarships in my future, I did improve with age: I became at least competitive at recreational volleyball and racquetball. I also work out twice a week with my trainer, a retired NFL player who (perhaps not coincidentally) has also volunteered to train kids with autism -- so it's a good fit in that sense! I pay for the entire time slot so that I can work out alone, a clear indicator of my social limitations. Although I would enjoy the competition of working out with my brother, for example, the mental annoyance of working out with strangers is just too high, and I wouldn't stick with it -- I've tried. Alone, I've been consistent for a decade straight. In my case, athletic development including coordination was slow and came later in life, but improvement does appear possible, leading me to believe that coordination and athletic ability are most accurately termed as "developmental delays," and not "deficits," that accompany autism.

I am a firm believer that athletic repetition and training are key for kids with autism to help counter the delays they naturally may face in movement, balance, and coordination -- the sooner it begins, the better. Study after study has confirmed that kids with autism benefit greatly from such training and respond rapidly. What I find especially interesting and encouraging are the studies that report improvement in comorbidities: as motor coordination, equilibrium, strength, and performance increase, so too do measurables in the psychosocial areas. In other words, physical training for kids on the autism spectrum seems to have behavioral benefits as well.

# Stimming

Stimming ("self-stimulating behavior") comes in many forms:

- Rocking
- Spinning
- Jumping
- Flapping hands
- Snapping Fingers
- Staring at lights or spinning objects as though in a trance
- Vocalizations
- Yelling
- Sniffing or other "tics"
- Repeating words or phrases or questions

Stimming is a frequent feature of autism, and it might be the first thing you observe about someone who has autism. One thing to keep in mind is that although stimming is very common amongst people with autism, it is not limited to them; the neurotypical often develop habits such as tapping their pencil, bouncing their knee, drumming their fingers, twirling their hair, and so on. With autism, however, the habits are simply much more pervasive and frequent.

As my most obvious example, I snap my fingers when I walk. The discovery of my own stimming led me to explore precisely why I do it. I believe that stimming is a form of self-calming for the nervous system, providing a predictable set of overt stimulations that override the continual onslaught of new mini stimuli as one walks down a hallway, for example. The experience of walking through the constantly changing visual and contextual landscape as you proceed is anchored by the consistency and predictability of the snapping. By engaging in stimming behavior, the experience of walking down the hallway takes on a familiar and predictable feel and the individual feels as though they are in control of this new experience to a certain extent.

Once stimming has been used in this manner enough times, it becomes naturally associated with the calming response, and many people with autism will exhibit stimming behaviors when managing fear, anxiety, excitement, or other strong emotions.

## Pathological or Preventative?

People with autism might use stimming effectively to help control and manage stress, anxiety, and strong emotions, but at some point, it may cross a line from helpful to problematic. For example, if a student with autism is compelled to wave their arms or yell out in class, it can be disruptive to the rest of the children. When evaluating whether stimming behaviors have become pathological or not, consider:

Does the stimming cause or increase social isolation?

Is the stimming disruptive to others in the school or workplace?

Is the stimming affecting their ability to learn or perform their job?

Is the stimming in any way dangerous or harmful?

If the drawbacks simply outweigh the benefits provided by the stimming, then strategies for minimizing or eliminating it should be considered. It's a personal choice, but in my opinion, stimming that does not draw significant unwanted attention or have other negative effects is fine. In my mind, it helps relax the nervous system, and it's not as though by breaking a stimming habit the individual with autism will become more resilient--if anything, the opposite will be true.

## Reducing Problematic Stimming

While someone with profound autism symptoms may never be able to (or may never desire to) entirely eliminate stimming behaviors, it may make sense to try to manage, reduce, or eliminate any stimming behaviors that are causing issues.

In children, punishment for stimming is generally discouraged, whereas encouraging and rewarding abstinence from it may be effective. To the extent that stimming is a form of releasing pent-up energy, increasing exercise has been shown to help, but it only goes so far.

I think that trying to stop all stimming would be a poor choice and may not be realistic. Better, perhaps, to modify or redirect the stimming in a way that still provides the benefit without distracting or disturbing others. In my own case, my compromise was to replace finger snapping with silent fingertip tapping (i.e., silent snapping, more or less). This allows me to continue the behavior without disturbing those around me.

Replacing stimming behaviors might also be an option; if a child with autism flaps their hands, perhaps squeezing a rubber stress ball will suffice. In some people, the drugs which increase available serotonin in the brain, selective serotonin reuptake inhibitors, or "SSRI"s, have shown themselves to be helpful in reducing stimming. That might lead us to the conclusion that stimming by itself also increases the levels of brain serotonin.

In conclusion, stimming is a self-calming technique that people with autism use to reduce anxiety and provided their stimming does not bring excess unwanted social attention or cause a distraction or disruption, seems otherwise harmless.

## Resistance to Change

Many people with autism are uncomfortable with changes in their environment and their circumstances, often willing to go to great lengths to avoid it whenever possible. There is an insistence upon sameness and strict adherence to routines. Unlike the stereotypical stick in the mud who cannot simply be bothered to keep up with trends and fashions, however, a person on the autism spectrum may find such change appealing on its merits while still experiencing some anxiety at the prospect of change.

## Why do Those with Autism Resist Change?

People on the spectrum can put a great deal of energy into avoiding change in part because change can be overstimulating and anxiety-inducing; changes also reduce the individual with autism's resilience and too much change can even lead to a meltdown if not well managed. But why? Fundamentally, what causes this resistance to change?

First, we should note that change comes in at least three forms: change in one's self, change in one's environment, and changes in one's circumstance. Each can cause significant stress to individuals with autism.

As we've seen, the resistance to changes in the environment -- such as losing a favorite place to sit -- is based in part on the amount of intellectual effort invested by the individual with autism: the effort spent in getting it right in the first place.

The sometimes-intense resistance to changes in one's circumstances can be harder for the neurotypical to understand. The most classic case might be the need to avoid separation from a loved one; perhaps it's as simple as the fact that emotional connections are very hard for individuals with autism to build in the first place, so again, anything that jeopardizes them places a huge amount of invested effort at risk. If emotional connections are difficult to establish, it makes sense that they will be even more precious.

Change also involves risk, and in my experience, while those with autism are not necessarily risk-averse per se, they often need to intellectually understand--and internally accept and agree to--the tradeoffs involved. It can be maddening to me to pick up an increase in risk with no attendant benefit. After all, why would you? Consider the simple case of introducing an exotic new food to my diet: if the thought of consuming a snail causes me anxiety, I must weigh that against the potential benefit of how great it might taste. And between you and me, I highly doubt that escargot is so delicious that the risk of eating snails is worth it. And so, I remain rigidly fixed amongst the snailless. I'd prefer yogurt and Sour Patch Kids*, thanks.

Perhaps one of the most basic reasons that people with autism fear change is that they may operate in a rule-based manner in certain areas of their lives. Because so much of human interaction fails to come naturally for them, they must instead build up a practiced repertoire of responses to various situations. Building this repertoire can take a lifetime, and change means that some percentage of what you know -- your rules system -- is now invalid. But which parts, and how do they get fixed?

And finally, at a simple level, change also means annoyance and irritation. In all these cases, the common denominator is anxiety -- anxiety over losing invested effort to a capricious external change, anxiety over the unknown of personal change and growth, anxiety over lost emotional connections, and anxiety over risk without reward.

There is much about social life that does not come naturally to some people with autism. Many aspects of it, such as the interplay of who looks where during the conversation, or who speaks next and at what point, are learned one at a time. They become rules or guidelines that the person with autism follows prescriptively to fit in and behave like everyone else. To deviate from them causes anxiety because it means the person is now operating outside known norms and must improvise, things

---

* A chewy candy

they know from experience that they are not traditionally good at. Hence, the individual with autism becomes very adept at--and even dependent upon--following a set of prescriptive rules, quickly spotting any exception that lay outside them, whether committed by themselves or others.

Plainly stated, then, many people with autism rigidly adhere to rituals, behaviors, and circumstances because the alternative -- accepting change -- may cause them intense anxiety. To move forward, the person with autism must learn to accept the annoyance and irritation associated with any important change. Hand in hand with any neurotypical partners involved, they must then work to face the anxiety and work through it.

# Secrets of the Autistic Millionaire

It's one thing to understand autism, and it's another thing to live with it, but it is something else entirely to live with and understand autism to the point that you can successfully master a life that has been encumbered with it.

The goal so far has been to educate and inform on autism, but in this section, we turn to the "secrets" of managing autism in a successful manner. This section contains the information that, by and large, I know now that I wish I had known earlier: the strategies and techniques that I now use to successfully manage and harness autism.

Imagine you were preparing a twelve-year-old boy with mild autism symptoms to spend the day fishing with his neurotypical uncle. You might have a series of tips for the uncle -- as simple as don't play the truck stereo too loudly until you see how he reacts, and so on. These are simple tips that make life easier for both parties. If you can make a day of fishing go more smoothly simply by providing some basic guidance, then it stands to reason that much of your daily life with autism might go more smoothly with a little information and preparation.

Beyond fishing are the deeper, more important life skills-- parenting, marriage, work, and so on. We shall look at and get advice on each of these from varying perspectives: the person with autism, the neurotypical partner, and so on. Along the way, we will discover the techniques that have enabled me to achieve and maintain a broad and varied success across my own life. Let's turn our attention now from the small details of life to the bigger topics: parenting, employment, and marriage.

## Autism and Autism on the Job

With my diagnosis not coming until after I retired early from Microsoft, it goes without saying that I spent my entire career largely oblivious to the fact that I was "different." In part, this is because the company I was working at, Microsoft, had so many other people that also exhibited autism symptoms that it really meant I fit in quite well most times! Although there were a great number of people not unlike me, it still made for a complicated landscape when it came to social interaction and management. Microsoft was very much an email culture and thus most of what we did every day could be done without face-to-face interaction, but even so, the deficits in social communication became problematic for me.

### The Autistic Employee

In my early days there, I would estimate that a quarter of the workforce at Microsoft was noticeably "on the spectrum." At that time most of the management was comprised of former developers who had been promoted to positions of leadership based largely on their technical achievements, which was also the situation in my own case. This promotion of technically successful programmers meant a lot of supervisors and leads were possibly on the spectrum as well.

Being an employee with autism can be challenging, particularly if you are not open about it. The sometimes-flat affect can cause others to jump to conclusions: people who really had not even met me would assume that I was grouchy, insubordinate, or rude -- until they got to know me. People with autism can take and deliver expressions too literally, be too blunt, make pointed remarks, and appear aloof or detached. These things complicate any relationship but are especially problematic in a coworker, where the relationship is different from that of family or friend.

Here are just a few of the basic ways in which autism can impact on-the-job performance; not each one is always a negative, but they all can have negative implications:

- Failure to make eye contact, smile, or follow other social conventions
- Interrupting; talking too slowly / quickly / loudly / quietly
- Missing sarcasm and taking things too literally
- Lack of flexibility, always needing to have something a certain way
- Unintentionally offending others with honest and direct statements
- Continuing to discuss a topic long past its freshness date, or continuing to ask questions after its clear question time is over
- Speaking to supervisors, managers, and owners without appropriate deference for the situation

- Problems controlling anger or frustration
- Advice incorrectly perceived or received as criticism
- May be gullible and subject to exploitation
- Ending conversations by simply turning or walking away
- Needing breaks in long meetings to "decompress" periodically
- Tendency to assign blame during conflict resolution
- Unable to successfully navigate office politics

If employees that have autism face so many challenges, then, why would a company such as Microsoft be so highly populated with them? There are many reasons why someone with autism can be a highly valuable employee; these are again generalizations and don't apply to every individual with autism symptoms, but in broad terms:

- Very strong logical and analytical skills
- Lack of social filters can be valuable for unvarnished truths
- Deep specialized knowledge in their field of expertise
- Creative problem solving
- Highly technically able
- Incredible perseverance in solving problems
- Excellent memory and detail recall, accuracy, attention to detail
- Love of structure, order, and even repetition
- Honesty, loyalty, predictability, reliability
- Thrive on routine

- Highly accountable to dates and milestones
- Self-motivated and driven to do well at whatever they are passionate about
- Highly conscientious

The inclusion of "lack of social filter" might surprise you, as it is truly a double-edged sword: it's a powerful ability to see through the social haze of niceties and extract the sometimes inconvenient or painful truth: consider the parable of the *Emperor's New Clothes*. It is the ability to say what everyone is thinking but afraid to say. There are, of course, significant attendant risks to such a lack of a filter!

## Central Coherence in Autistic Employees

Neurotypical people, particularly those with high central coherence, like to organize their tasks and work into neat groups and tie them up with a bow, whereas those with autism tend to have weaker coherence and can tend to get bogged down in the details.

Difficulties with central coherence may manifest themselves as difficulty with organization, such as:

- Trouble getting started because they don't know where to begin
- A perpetually disorganized or messy desk or workspace
- Difficulty following multi-step directions or plans
- Needing assistance in setting priorities to organize tasks and deliverables

- Not being able to accurately estimate how long a project should take
- Becoming overwhelmed by interruptions and annoyances
- Becoming too rigorously locked into a particular plan or way of thinking
- Act impulsively too early on before a complete plan is formulated
- Asking too many clarifying questions

Clearly, there is no one template, and any such challenges are complications and not limitations!

# "Fitting In" vs Being Accommodated at Work

In the social arena, people with autism that do not attempt to adjust their behavior to fit in with the accepted norms will find themselves ostracized to a certain extent. Other people will simply choose not to be around you if your behavior is too different, particularly if it is annoying to them in some dimension. In a work environment, however, the other people simply don't have a choice. They're required to stay at their posts even if they find you incredibly annoying! This can lead to resentment at a minimum.

Fundamentally, the best advice I can give here is to pick your battles carefully. If you have an aspect of your behavior or personality that is causing friction or problems at work, you need to carefully consider how attached you are to it. If it is a fundamental cornerstone of who you are, you may well refuse to adapt. But in all the other ways in which you can make it easier for others to get along with you, why not? We visit the question of fitting in a later section.

## The Autistic Manager

It was only in the years after retiring that I began to look back at my career and what it meant to me. Landing the job at Microsoft all the way from Saskatchewan had been a major psychological vindication that I was the real deal, more than merely a lucky imposter. As is typical in most companies, good performance was met with advancement, and in the first decade I progressed up through the ranks from intern to Software Design Engineer to Lead Developer and ultimately Development Manager. In retrospect, however, while my performance might have merited the advancement, my management skills did not match my technical ability. I might have been a natural-born coder, but that certainly did not make me a natural-born leader or manager!

I took several classes internally at work to learn about some of the challenges of managing others -- thinking that my quirky personality might make it difficult for others to "get" me. Perhaps the most helpful to me were the ones that emphasized different styles of personality. The moment I had let go of the delusion that everyone would want to be managed exactly as I would like to be, I realized just how different each of the various personality types is, and how their needs vary in such an organization. This is a real challenge for someone with any degree of mindblindness.

I had only sought out the extra training because I sensed that I had a personal deficit -- I had not managed people before, and it seemed a weakness, so I wanted to get training in that area – – and not because I had autism (which I still had no idea of yet). The key, I believe, for any manager with autism is to make the effort to accommodate all the various personality, learning, and operational styles in your organization. What works for you personally will likely not be an effective strategy for managing others. Your own needs are almost certainly very different from the neurotypical employee, so using them to predict what your staff needs would be foolish.

Once I had accepted that people had very different styles in terms of how they operated within the company and what they needed for affirmation and direction, I could adapt my management of each employee to their own unique needs and style. Or at least, I could try!

If I had it all to do over again, and if my autism were serious enough to be noticeable to my subordinates (as mine is, I believe), and if at the time I enjoyed the luxury of knowing that I had autism, I would certainly tell my employees that I was on the spectrum. Why? Because I think knowing the context of why my reactions are going to be different than other managers could be helpful.

One of the biggest challenges for a new manager with autism is the shift in focus away from their area of expertise. In my case, I went from a highly technical role to a management role. Dealing with the social and personal issues of a group of employees is *very* different than solving a complex technical challenge off in a corner by yourself. Dealing well with irrationality might be completely new to you! Office politics can also be a challenge, as when you move up the corporate ladder, you wind up operating in a new political sphere as well -- whether you realize it or not.

Another option is to simply resist the drift into management if you can do so without scuttling your career financially. Even in a company as technically focused as Microsoft, there was an almost-inexorable push towards management as you went up the career ladder. I say "almost", however, because for those with the technical ability to pull it off, an "individual contributor" role, where they remain technically focused, might be a better choice. It is a more demanding path technically, but for certain personality types, the most rewarding. After all, when I was a kid riding my bike down to Radio Shack it was because I was fascinated with computers and programming, not with meetings and PowerPoint presentations!

## Working for an Autistic Manager

If you are working for someone you believe has autism, particularly if you are neurotypical, you are going to face several unique challenges. But how can you even know whether your boss is on the spectrum, especially if they have never been tested? One cannot assume that every introverted technical person has autism -- it's simply not the case. And so, the reality is that you may only suspect that your boss is on the spectrum without ever being able to confirm it authoritatively.

Imagine for a moment that your boss has a diagnosis and has been kind enough to inform you of it; then you can begin to try to make the necessary adjustments. The problem is, without really knowing the person, how can you know which kinds of things are important to them or that they might be sensitive about? Are there things you can do to increase the odds of your success, such as not wearing strong perfume to work perhaps, or not flipping on the fluorescent lights in their office each time you walk in or rearranging old things in a new way?

Odds are if you work for someone in a technical arena that has autism, that person will be very well versed in that field. They likely have deep knowledge of the area in which they are most passionate; in fact, it's quite possible that their knowledge level and the rate at which they can take in and assimilate new information about it is far above your own. And equally frequently, these individuals will be straightforward and direct -- if they know the answer to your question, and there's a high chance they will -- you will get that answer with a minimum of sideshow. More than simply a manager, they might also be a great resource to you.

If your boss has autism and their eye contact is affected, keep in mind that the normal signals one might read from inconsistent eye contact such as intimidation or disinterest do not apply; those with autism have their own cadence to their eye contact, depending on how significant their symptoms are and how hard they've worked (or not worked) to address it. Don't take it personally!

A boss with autism might not be as tuned in to the office politics and social structure as a neurotypical individual might be, and you can assist them in that regard by being direct and straightforward yourself. You might even find a role for yourself as a translator of sorts: perhaps subtly letting them know what's going on in your team, one level deeper than they can see into the neurotypical world of personal wants, desires, hurt feelings, and egos.

People with autism often are much more literal about what they say than others. To that end, you too should say what you mean, mean what you say--be literal yourself. Take dates and facts seriously, as they do. If you regularly pepper your speech with sarcasm and irony, you might have to dial that back for your boss. A dry wit, in particular, can be misread entirely.

You may also have to resolve yourself to some brutally honest feedback. A manager with autism may not couch his or her negative feedback as gently as a neurotypical manager would. You will need to receive that as it is intended -- a factual evaluation and not a personal slight. As a generalization, they tend to avoid being passive-aggressive. Positive feedback from a manager with autism can be the sweetest currency of all because you know it is so literal and direct -- praise from a manager with autism probably results from a job well done and not some attempt to manipulate you.

It is unlikely that an individual with autism who has trouble controlling their emotions in the workplace would be promoted to a position where it becomes a significant liability, but it *can* happen. In such cases, if a manager with autism becomes unduly upset, I recommend time and distance; give them space. Arguing with them or trying to resolve it factually in the moment might not be the most productive approach, as the manager may simply need time to sort themselves emotionally before they are able to continue logically. No amount of logic will necessarily short circuit that process.

A manager with autism might even seem rude at times--not using proper deference towards upper management, interrupting conversations to get a point in, simply walking away at the end of a hallway conversation, and so on. These are deficiencies in their social abilities to be sure, but you'll do better not to take them personally, as they are not intended as such. They are truly oversights from not knowing better or not understanding why such things are deemed important.

Odds are that as you spend time working for someone with autism you will come to find there are a few things -- like punctuality or order, perhaps -- that seem disproportionately important to them. What those things are vary from one individual to the next, but those with autism tend to hold a few core concepts in very high regard, such as perhaps the notion that punctuality is a direct placeholder for respect. If you are perpetually tardy, a manager with autism may come to see that as disrespect or even insubordination, depending on how passionate they are about it. To you, it might be a simple five-minute delay at the beginning of meetings, but to them, it might be symbolic of the entire relationship between the two of you. Assuming that they will get over it and move on is likely a poor bet. They tend not to.

The issues surrounding employment and autism are many and complex, and we have but touched the surface of a topic that could easily support a book on its own! Ultimately, the goal should be to have an individual with autism fully engaged in their passion in such a way that their goals are aligned with those of the company. With those aligned, much of the rest will begin to fall into place as long as care and attention are paid to the many emotional, social, and interpersonal relationships that are created along the way, both with other employees and with customers.

## Parenting with Autism

Imagine being a regimented perfectionist who is quick to anger, doesn't suffer fools gladly, likes peace and quiet, and who reads emotions poorly, dwelling in the tiny details and ignoring the big picture. Now add four little kids and stir. Welcome to family life with autism!

This is not about children that have autism, but rather it focuses on being the parent with autism. I simply would not be able to write effectively about parenting a child with autism as it is something that I have never done, and my own experience as having been a child with autism is simply not enough context for me to attempt it. I know nothing of the challenges faced, dreams altered, and let's be frank -- the potential heartache -- that can accompany an autism diagnosis in a child and would not attempt to advise another parent.

### Being the "Other" Parent

Before we examine the challenges in being a parent with autism, we should acknowledge the unique challenges of being the neurotypical parent in a mixed marriage with kids. There is simply a certain set of things that the partner with autism may not be good at -- let's say something as simple as phoning to schedule appointments for the baby with the pediatrician's office. If the partner with autism isn't comfortable on the phone, the neurotypical partner may wind up picking up that role by default.

This only works, of course, if the partner with autism picks up other responsibilities and roles in the parenting arena that, in turn, compensate for or take work off the shoulders of the neurotypical parent. It's one thing to be the "other" parent and a completely different thing to be the *only* parent. And if I might be blunt, no matter how much the partner with autism doesn't like the phone (or whatever the task in question may be), parents simply must accept that they will be called upon to do many, *many* things that they aren't good at, that they have no prior experience with, and that they will find distasteful. It's part of the job, so you might as well get used to it on *both* sides.

The best you can do is distribute the work fairly in a way that plays to each of your strengths. The notion that all work that is not aligned with the skills of the partner with autism must all fall to the neurotypical partner is a non-starter, as there is simply too much of it! Remember that much of it isn't likely to come naturally to either party.

With the workload distributed as fairly as possible, the neurotypical partner may still wind up at times feeling like a solo parent as they often must attempt to accommodate and integrate the sometimes-inflexible demands and routines and expectations on the part of the partner with autism. That parent may also have trouble accepting the new levels of noise, mess, disorder, and interruption that they are not accustomed to. They may have invested a lifetime in building and maintaining a certain semblance of order and structure in their lives only to have it suddenly demolished by a crying baby or rowdy teen.

I am also a firm believer that in the case of your kids, you do what you can even when it's not enough. For example, in my children's school careers, I calculate there have been likely two parent-teacher conferences per year, per kid, for ten years each, starting in preschool. That's about eighty opportunities to meet with various teachers (granted, many at the same school on the same day), but let's call it forty to make it manageable. My wife would schedule them, and even when I was working full time, I made the effort to be present even if Nicole was charged with driving the agenda and running the meetings from a social perspective. I could still smile and nod and flip through to inspect the textbook, ask a few questions, and be invested in my kid's outcome. Let us say that as a highly devoted working parent, I made it to thirty of those. Rest assured that Nicole still made it to all of them -- as the "other" parent in a mixed autistic partnership, you simply might have to.

I repay what I can of this imbalance in other areas of our lives, and it is not enough to be the primary breadwinner -- so I am trusted with the alarm systems, audio-visual, telephone, Wi-Fi, network, and other systems; I'm the only one who knows how the lids come off the septic tanks or how to unclog the pipes; the only human that ventures into the literal crawlspace where the basement furnace lives or where the pool pumps hide; changes the oil in and otherwise maintains the cars; runs the generators; goes up on the roof as needed; does pressure washing in the spring and other similar things that I am personally good at. Hopefully, you can find a delineation between roles in your own relationship that evenly splits the workload *and* leverages the differing abilities of each parent in a useful fashion.

# Being a Good Parent with Autism

Being a good parent with autism can be challenging at the best of times. That may sound like some unabashed pessimism, particularly coming from a father of four, but it is really rooted in caution: I am extremely fortunate in that all my kids have turned out healthy, happy, smart, and well adjusted, but I honestly believe that is, to a certain extent, despite my autism (and thanks to my amazing wife). Had I known then what I know now, I could have made much better adjustments, but it is only now, with a late-life diagnosis, that I can look back at my parenting experience and draw any conclusions. I still have two teenagers at home, so for me it's not too late to make improvements!

Here is a partial list of the characteristics that can make parenting even more challenging than it already would be for the neurotypical; naturally everyone is different, which makes this (like most lists) a gross generalization. This list includes many parallels to the issues we see in the "Autistic Manager" section, but with parenting, you have the added complexity of almost complete authority over your charges.

- Perfectionism
- Regimentation
- Quick-tempered
- Low tolerance for noise and annoyance
- Tendency to see new friends as home "invaders"
- Open and frank responses to situations without a social filter regardless of the audience present
- May often look sad or angry in their facial expressions

- Poor cognitive shifting from one issue to another, possibly more important one
- Compromised ability to read intent and motives
- Decreased ability to read the child's emotions and to intuit their emotional needs
- Feedback/correction can be too critical/literal
- Infrequent positive feedback and praise
- Difficulty communicating with teachers and others involved in child's life

## The Perils of Assuming Motive and Intent

As a parent, you are the local constabulary and the criminal justice system at the same time -- you are both law *and* order. Correctly interpreting what a child *intended* to do can be extremely important in deciding whether a child is culpable for any particular action.

From a simple behavioral standpoint, accidentally bumping a flower vase is quite different than maliciously pushing it over to destroy it, and each merits a very different response. Parenting that seems arbitrary and capricious -- where accidental events are wrongly attributed as intentional just a little too often -- no doubt becomes increasingly frustrating for the child. I am no child development expert, but I would imagine it's difficult to grow up in a learning structure where the conclusions drawn about your actions are generally wrong. I'm sure I have made many errors in this regard over time; it's a real risk that accompanies mindblindness.

In my own case, the compromise is often for me to admit that often I simply do not know what has actually happened. To frame it in a hypothetical: I can ask what happened, and I can say what the consequences will be if an action is repeated, but I do make a significant effort to not draw conclusions that I cannot prove. Thus, I wind up saying things like "I don't know who spilled the lemonade, but… (here's why it matters and here's what'll happen next time)." Yes, this runs this risk of the parent coming away looking a little foolish for perhaps not knowing exactly what's going on, but I think that's preferable to risking an environment that feels unjust for the child.

## Emotional Blind Spots

I am fortunate in that children tend to telegraph, not hide, their emotions. I'm further fortunate that I can read facial expressions reasonably well, so if I can see my child's face, I can then know the context of what is happening, I have a fairly tuned in view of what they are feeling.

That said, there are times my wife needs to explain a nuance to me, such as *why* something might be important to a child. It's not that I'm often wrong, but I'm occasionally unaware. My own tendency will be to look at the situation, gather all the information, and make an informed decision about how I would feel if I were in that position. As helpful as that dance can be in daily life, it's less helpful when dealing with small children because their priorities are different, their maturity level is different, and their thought process is different. My middle-aged brain is a terrible proxy for the wants and needs of a two-year-old. Sometimes leaning on the neurotypical parent for more perspective, if you can, will really open your eyes to the complexity of what might be going on with the child at any particular moment.

## Remember that Kids are Children

Not to be overly pedantic about this, but kids really *are* immature little children. They will act as such: loud, annoying, and unpredictable in all their rule-breaking, change-making glory. Kids can test the patience of even the most understanding of adults, and if you are the sort of person who has prided themselves on not putting up with a lot of nonsense in the past, get ready for some serious nonsense!

Some people would find it a lot easier to put up with a troublesome pet than a toddler in their "terrible twos," and if you're one of them, you need to consider the reasons why a child triggers a negative emotion within you that a dog does not. Perhaps it stems from perceived intent: a child's action might pique your temper because they should know better, whereas a Labrador retriever doesn't have a clue, so it's easier for you to let a transgression go and move on. If this notion resonates with you, this is where again I stress that children are *not* merely small adults. They make choices in ways that will sometimes flummox you, but you must not fall prey to the trap of assuming intent if you have autism and any degree of mindblindness.

First, their brains are different, not solely because their frontal cortex -- which associates future outcomes with present actions -- is terribly immature and undeveloped. Sometimes they will even intentionally take or select the wrong action merely to explore the consequences. It's hard to anticipate the mind of a toddler.

Second, with mindblindness, even if you were prepared to *accept* the internal motives and intents that drive a toddler, it doesn't mean you can perceive and receive that intent accurately. Imagine for a moment that your baby daughter flips her spaghetti bowl upside down and onto the floor while you aren't looking: the possibilities are endless. She might have just been uncoordinated and dropped it while moving it or perhaps she was startled and bumped it off the tray. But there's always the slight chance that she did it just for laughs and to watch you clean it up at the end of an already long day. If your response to the situation would vary markedly on how you interpreted the child's intent, you will be facing some serious challenges. Your responses need to be a function of the *situation*, not your *mood*.

Raising children with mindblindness means two things: you will never intuitively know what your child's motives behind any choice or action were, but your attempts to guess, infer or assign motive are ineffective and doomed to failure--unless you make an intentional effort *not* to assume motive.

## Remembering Your Children's Friends

I'm terrible with names and faces, which means I find it hard to remember the names of even my children's close friends until I've seen them enough times. It does me no good to know "This is Daniel." Even seeing Daniel, a half-dozen times and hearing his name might not do it. But if I know that Daniel plays running back for the high school football team and that he's number 32 on the roster, I can usually associate the face and name with "running back" and in a little time, they will come naturally as well. If you suffer from some prosopagnosia (trouble remembering faces), let your children know it extends to *all* people, lest they assume you cannot remember their friends because they are somehow less important!

## Intruder Alert! Intruder Alert!

People with autism often view new visitors to the home that they do not know with a certain "intruder sense." It's not a judgment on the actual individual, as it has nothing to do with them per se, it's really about the sense that something is different and someone else has entered the sanctity of the family home. This is not to say that when my kids have friends over that I become concerned that something will be damaged or stolen: my kids' friends are great people. I merely experience a certain level of angst and irritation from the fact that things are different, and the normal course of daily family life is now operating under different rules and has a different "feel" due to the presence of guests in the home. Since we know that people with autism often are uncomfortable with change in general, new people in the home represent a very personal form of change.

## Accepting Change and Disorder

As someone with autism, I like things the way I like them. I don't want people messing with the carefully crafted reality that I've set up around me, especially after I've managed to get everything in my life arranged "just so." Kids will absolutely create unwanted change and disorder in your life, and you cannot blame them for this unavoidable fact. You're going to have to learn to roll with it to a certain extent. I realize that telling you, "It's inevitable -- suck it up!" doesn't sound helpful at first, but I'm being intentionally blunt because I truly believe this is one of those things in life you just must accept as a fact of life: kids will introduce some chaos into your life, and it's not their fault that they're kids. You need to be able to accept a certain amount of disruption.

That said, as we discuss in the chapter on accommodations, there are many things that the family, the spouse, and the autistic parent can do to help mitigate the impacts of this chaos.

Having a quiet spot that is your own can help a great deal. I have an office with a computer, as well as a workshop that I can retreat to in order to decompress when the social demands of having people over and the intruder sense become a bit overwhelming.

When my oldest child reached his teen years, his voice and the voices of his friends changed, sounding more like men. When they stayed up later than I did, I found it increasingly difficult to sleep with the voices of other adult men in the home -- noise-canceling headphones became increasingly useful.

## Being Candid with Your Children

By the time I was diagnosed, my oldest son was already twenty years old, so being open about my autism with my eldest kids when they were at a younger age wasn't an option that was open to me at the time. Since my diagnosis, however, I have discussed it with my younger (teen and pre-teen) children extensively. If you have such a diagnosis, I suggest you share it with your children as soon as you believe they are ready.

Here are some of the topics I suggest you address if you do have a discussion with your children:

## Autistic Parents and Change

Change can be hard. People with autism prefer things to follow certain routines, and they can become anxious or irritated when there is an unexpected change in plans. If you break a rule or do something else that brings unexpected change for an autistic parent, you may wish to wait for them to process or cope with that change before talking to them about the specifics, if possible. If we are in the middle of driving to X and something happens to scuttle that plan, I might react more strongly than the situation merits, simply because I dislike changing plans.

## Considerations for Socializing and for Having Friends Over

A parent with autism may not see the need to socialize as much as the kids do, and hence they may find it strange how much the kids want and need to do so. We know that an autistic parent may be reluctant to have routines disrupted by having their kids' friends over, plus any new guest may be seen as an intruder or invader of sorts until they become used to it. But remember, even things that are new and weird to a parent with autism can become normal over time if done in a way so as not to cause undue stress. Making the process of having new friends over into a "normal" thing will benefit everyone involved.

Depending on the family's preference and the situation at hand, you might wish to explain to your friend that your parent has autism, and as a result is more sensitive than most to noise, disruption, and interruption. The explanations need not go any deeper than you wish.

## Keep it Down

As described earlier, a parent with autism is likely a lot more sensitive to certain sensory irritations, like loud or annoying sounds. All parents will inevitably ask you to keep it down saying, "Turn that music down!" and such, but the tolerance threshold for autistic parents is likely to be a lot lower. For the parent with autism, once the kids are older and you can afford the distraction, I recommend noise-canceling headphones. I'm wearing a pair\* right now. They do not eliminate the sound entirely but reduce and soften it, making it less distracting and less stressful.

As noted, falling asleep with loud male voices in the home is still nigh impossible for me, as I imagine a crying baby might keep others up, so I do need a *certain* amount of quiet past bedtime.

## Meeting New Friends

Kids are often mortified by their own parents and at certain ages can come to view parents as embarrassing relics that have to be introduced to their friends only out of necessity. Don't

---

\* I recommend the Bose "over the ear" style headphones with active noise cancellation!

take it personally, and don't assume it has anything to do with your autism when it does happen -- it seems most kids get that way, least briefly, in their teen years. Presuming that you are doing your best to be friendly and welcoming to their friends, your obligation there is largely met.

If the symptoms of your autism are readily apparent when someone first meets you because they affect your speech or movement in a way that makes you stand out from neurotypical individuals, remember that kids -- especially teens and pre-teens -- crave normality. They do not want to stand out and be identified as different for any reason -- including the reason of having an autistic parent. Your child might be temporarily embarrassed by you, and it's easy to take offense at that. Remember, however, that almost *all* kids are embarrassed by their parents at that age, and your situation is thus hardly unique. It will pass, and it's a stage of normal childhood development, not about you.

## Timing and Expectations

The timing of friend visits and parties can also be important to me. When my kids became older teens, it took me a long time before I was able to go to bed before them while they stayed up.

If I'm told earlier that there will be a party/event/gathering from seven until ten o'clock, it can become stressful for me if it runs substantially longer, off-plan. The unknown and unexpected can act as "stress multipliers" on top of the disruption from normal routines. When things do go off-plan, remember that it impacts the person with autism more profoundly and differently than you might expect it to.

No social event goes entirely according to plan, but at least in my case, the more I know in advance and the closer things do go to plan, the better. My own task becomes to roll with as much change and novelty as I can while the family around me tries to minimize the impact of any significant disruptions.

If a social event we are hosting goes long, which is more than about three to four hours for myself (everyone is different), I sometimes need to excuse myself, retreat to my workshop, den, or bedroom, and just "be away from it all" for a while. As we discuss in the chapter on masking, maintaining any kind of performance for hours on end can be demanding. Sometimes a break makes a big difference.

When we go out to an event, particularly a family event for kids at the school or similar, it places quite a demand on me. That's not to say that I do not enjoy it or would rather be elsewhere, but it does mean that it's work -- I have a fixed capacity for doing it, even when it's enjoyable.

There are times I should excuse myself, at least temporarily, but have failed to do so, which makes it even harder on me. For example, I have three boys that play football, and all have gone through the same local high school program. Each year for three years for three kids -- almost ten years now -- I've attended their annual youth football awards banquet. It's always planned for two hours but regularly goes well past four, as each kid is thoughtfully spoken of and every adult in the program receives some well-deserved recognition. Because it's a worthy thing, it's never cut short, and I'm not arguing it should be. For me, however, four hours in a chair at a banquet table listening to speeches about people I don't know is a real test of how much I love my kids! By the third hour, I'd (literally) rather be smashing rocks with a hammer out in the parking lot, but I do love them, so I'll be there next year as well.

My strategy for when we go out to similar school functions or banquets is to be aware of this three-hour reserve capacity. If an event goes to four hours or more, I likely need to start considering accommodations that will allow me to take a break or leave early. Because this is not a normal need it wasn't something we recognized early, but as discussed in the chapter on accommodations, now we know that *everyone* will be happier if we manage to keep Dad at least reasonably comfortable.

Parenting with autism is a complex topic. Your best bet, I contend, would be to keep your primary goal in the forefront of your mind: that you wish to develop your children into healthy, happy, functional, and self-supporting adults. Sometimes a lack of strong central coherence can cause an autistic parent to lose sight of the big goal and to become distracted by temporary annoyances. By doing your best to keep your focus on the overall objective, the surprises and annoyances that do inevitably come along will be a lot less distracting.

## Love and Relationships with Autism

If I have any qualifications for writing about a successful marriage when autism is involved, they begin with the fact that I have been happily married to my high school sweetheart for over twenty-five years. It is challenging enough to maintain a great marriage over a long period of time, and even more so when the couple is young when they meet. As people change so much in young adulthood, more times than not they grow apart, and not together, over time.

Adding autism to the complications which can beset a marriage is one thing, but to have an autistic partner who has not yet been diagnosed -- or worse, is autistic but does not believe themselves to be--can make for quite a challenge. Such was the case in my own marriage, as we spent those first twenty-five years without a diagnosis -- I suppose we just thought I was just "Dave", and as such Dave was a little different and needed certain accommodations.

People with autism are also at a significantly increased risk of depression, anxiety, obsessive-compulsive disorder, and attention deficit disorder. The odds are that if you've been dealing with undiagnosed autism, perhaps you've also been managing one or more of these other aspects without knowing what is underpinning them -- autism itself.

I am no exception, and we have had to contend with each of these at one time or another (except for obsessive-compulsive disorder). That we did so for decades without even knowing they were even related is a testament to the strength of our marriage, the character of Nicole, my wife, and the effort we put forth together.

The simple statistical fact that autism is about four times more common in males than females means that the majority of the "mixed marriages" will involve a woman in the neurotypical role married to a man with autism.

## The Courtship Stage

One interesting complaint I have seen leveled regarding (usually failed) relationships with a person with autism is that they were "faking it" from the start -- that the individual with autism had learned, from movies and books and television, how to mimic the important human courtship rituals, but once the marriage was consummated and the prize was won, the person with autism no longer had to try anymore, and the relationship fizzled out. That's a cynical description of anyone's relationship, but it argues for a longer pre-marriage engagement if nothing else!

Many autistic men without a diagnosis will fit the mold of someone who is kind, highly attentive, smart, and maybe a little bit immature -- not a bad combination in your late teens or early 20s when playing the relationship game. This can be further enhanced because the individual with autism's apparent intellect and abilities may speak to extensive career opportunities. The person with autism will also, no doubt, pay a high degree of attention to their partner during courtship.

Some have speculated that the limited social abilities, slight immaturity, and "strong silent type" aspect might trigger maternal compensation in some women as well. The neurotypical partner may see an initial blossoming in the autistic partner as they begin to open up, and perhaps overestimate how long that blossoming will continue, or how far it will go. They may believe the candidate's limited social abilities stem solely from problems in childhood and that love will conquer all given time.

Men with autism -- even undiagnosed -- often seek women who can compensate for their difficulties in daily life. For example, although it was not by conscious plan, as a highly introverted person I married an extremely gregarious and extroverted neurotypical woman. Anecdotally, and for reasons not entirely clear, women with autism are often said to look for a partner more like themselves.

In some cases, the person with autism may have created -- whether they are aware of it or not -- an internal "shopping list" that comprises the ideal relationship candidate and they will then go through life vetting potential partners against this list. Often at the top of the list will be those qualities an individual with autism is deficient in -- superior social and executive function. When someone matching the criteria is met, the full determination of the person with autism can be brought to bear, and such determination can be compelling.

My own case was no exception. Between serious relationships, I dated a half dozen women before meeting my future wife, but after finally getting to know her, I knew in my heart that she was "the one." Once that certainty had been triggered, I undertook my mission as doggedly as anything else I ever achieved in life. There have been times in our marriage where, perhaps at an event when Nicole looks exceptionally beautiful, that I will look across the room and be struck by what feels like love at first sight all over again. The next thought to cross my mind, however, is always predictable: *I will make her mine -- mission accepted*. No question. It's a mental resolution and decision that is made before my conscious brain can even remind itself -- typically to its own great relief -- that I've been married to her for decades already!

## The Subtle Social Dance

Even though there are certain issues, such as masking during testing, that I believe affect females with autism differently than males with autism, I have largely tried to avoid treating the genders differently in this book. When it comes to courtship, however, there can be no denying that eons of biological and cultural evolution have set a complex stage upon which the performers must tread. The roles are very different for men than they are for women, and each faces its own set of unique challenges.

Consider the all-important moment of the good-night kiss when the evening is coming to a close. Let's imagine that I'm a single adult male on the spectrum and that the girl asks me to come up for coffee. I'm not a complete fool -- I know it's late and people don't drink caffeine late at night so it's likely a euphemism for "come on upstairs and let's explore the sexual opportunities."

If, however, the girl asked something more subtle -- perhaps today she would suggest that we "watch some Netflix and chill," I would likely demur because I generally have an early schedule, and people really *do* stay up late and binge-watch Netflix. Instead, I would go home to post-process, if I were to then Google the phrase "Netflix and chill," I'd then discover that I had just turned down what was likely an explicit overture for sex. The specific lingo and verbiage change and evolve over time, but the fact that people are indirect about sex does not. And indirect does not serve people on the spectrum very well.

Nothing about human courtship is obvious or direct and that places those on the spectrum at a very distinct disadvantage. When I initially sensed that I was truly falling in love with Nicole it was more than thirty years before my autism diagnosis. Even so, I was self-aware enough to know that I wasn't quite like everyone else emotionally, either. To that end I told her something that remains true to this day, I think I told her, "You will have to go first." In the dance of life, I would have to let her lead emotionally. I don't really know where we're going, so I let her take me by the hand and lead me around this emotional life.

Dating, courtship, and romance are vastly more complicated for people on the spectrum for the very basic reason that so much of it is subtle, silent, unspoken communication -- the very specific area in which our most profound social deficits can be found.

## Common Problems Facing Mixed-Autism Couples

The most common cause of issues that I have identified amongst autistic couples with one autistic partner is an overestimation, on the part of the neurotypical partner, of how much the autistic partner will be able to change, adapt, or improve after marriage. Sometimes the initial effort put forth by the individual with autism, so impressive in the early stages, will fade after the honeymoon period when the motivation to be social is reduced or removed. Since socialization can be hard work for the autistic partner, they may simply (and unfairly) choose to entirely avoid it, forcing the neurotypical partner to adopt some of the lifestyle characteristics of autism into their own lives, often unwillingly.

The problem that the most common cause is a sense of isolation and loneliness in the neurotypical partner. A person with autism may be perfectly fine left to their own devices for hours or even days at a time, but this can be downright emotionally painful for a social person to endure, and it's unreasonable to expect either partner to wholly adopt the lifestyle instincts of the other.

## Asymmetrical Affection

Another common issue in mixed-autism relationships is an asymmetrical level of affection displayed by the two partners. Most relationships and marriages flourish best when there is an equal, or reciprocal, exchange of regular expressions of love and affection. Many with autism struggle with verbal expressions of their love and affection; even though they may feel it deeply, converting it into words is for some reason hard to do, and because it is so difficult, they avoid doing it often enough.

Those with autism also often strive for accuracy and consistency; to them, it might be perfectly sufficient to proclaim their love one time; it is now an established fact, one that has been plainly stated and need not be revisited repeatedly unless something changes. For the person with autism, frequently restating or reiterating the known and obvious can seem weird and even disingenuous; unfortunately, this will be very unsatisfying for the neurotypical partner.

Perhaps most telling is a recent survey (of women only) who are in a relationship with a partner with high-functioning autism. When asked "Does your partner love you?", fully 50 percent replied with "I do not know." This uncertainty results from an absence of regular, daily, tangible expressions of love. Too often the autistic partner will reply with logical communication of emotions such as "You know that I love you" or "I fixed the dishwasher, didn't I?" and leave it to the neurotypical partner to try to assemble some relationship scaffolding from it, but it's often too little to work with. Acts of service and logic are certainly compelling evidence but do not scratch the particular itch of being reaffirmed in the manner that the neurotypical partner needs to be fulfilled and happy.

While individuals with autism who enter marriages generally report being satisfied, happy, and less stressed afterward, the neurotypical partners often feel emotionally exhausted and neglected in the years later. This disconnect is not acceptable and explains in many cases why the partner with autism might be oblivious to the problems in the marriage. It could come as a complete surprise that there even is an issue to be addressed.

People with autism who might start out as not romantic by nature can further complicate their relationships by not understanding the importance of sexual intimacy (particular as distinct from mere sexual activity). The person with autism may not understand the value of, and need for, the back-and-forth, cat-and-mouse games of sexual tension, of play, of the value of being picked as the one special partner let into the secret garden, of an amorous atmosphere, foreplay, and of cuddling after.

I have elsewhere argued that people with autism spend a lifetime assembling a portfolio of prior experiences that teach them how to act in various circumstances because it does not come naturally. If this is true, then one can imagine that the source material for an individual with autism who has had limited relationship experience is primarily soap operas, movies, and pornography! Unfortunately, none of these are perfect representations of healthy human relationships from which the individual with autism can learn mastery.

Remember, however, that any highly functioning autistic partner has already mastered dozens, if not hundreds, of subtle social and relationship behaviors. Many more can be learned. Like so many of the other deficits related to this disorder, once the individual is aware of and understands the import, they can often address it.

## The Bucket Metaphor

One metaphor for explaining the differences between how people with autism process love and affection vs the neurotypical is to compare a bucket and coffee cup. The neurotypical carry around a bucket that they need to fill with love, and once it is full, they are generally content to carry it around, but it takes a lot to fill it. Those with autism operate with a coffee cup that must be refilled much more frequently with smaller doses. They themselves may operate, however, completely opposite to this, with the autistic partner being the one to treat affection and affirmation as if it were a logical asked-and-answered proposition of fact that need not be oft-repeated.

It is a safe bet for the individual with autism to assume that the neurotypical partner's bucket is never full and that there will always be room for more. Similarly, it would be hard for the neurotypical individual to "top off" the coffee cup of the autistic partner too often.

## Sexual Desire

Just as some with autism turn to computers, trains, dinosaurs, or astronomy as a special interest, some turn to sex. Some with autism may turn to pornography as their special interest, or as an authoritative relationship guide. Furthermore, in such cases, the desire for sexual activities and sexual intimacy can be excessive or even compulsive. These instances, however, are by far the exception and not the norm with autism. In fact, typically with autism, it is the neurotypical partner who is most concerned with a lack of sexual desire in the autistic partner, and certainly not an excess.

Some with autism can view sex as purely a practical activity for the purposes of reproduction, and once children are produced, the need or desire for sexual acts atrophies for them, causing significant problems in the relationship. If sex is viewed by the autistic partner as a primarily practical act or as the means to producing a family, once the family is in place, the need for sexuality logically diminishes. Equally logical, however, is the fact that sex remains an important ongoing factor in a successful relationship -- so too for the other partner.

Critically, willingness and availability are not replacements for enthusiasm. For the individual with autism to begrudgingly agree to more sex likely will not help things much, for it is the emotional recharge of being chosen that the neurotypical lacks, and not primarily the physical act. Better that they should seek it out with passion half as often rather than simply acquiescing more frequently.

## Mothering and Asymmetrical Responsibility

If the individual with autism lacks sufficient executive function, many roles fall squarely -- and solely -- onto the shoulders of the neurotypical individual, as we have seen. This partner can wind up taking on all responsibility for family finances, budgeting, planning, and so on. If all this is not their forte, significant additional stress arises. At the same time, if the individual with autism doesn't pick up a similar level of responsibility in other areas, a neurotypical female partner may begin to develop a "mothering" role in caring for the person with autism rather than forming a true partnership.

Whatever the reason, women who are married to autistic men report that their partner originally reminded them of their fathers even more so than in neurotypical marriages.

## The Autism Diagnosis

As stressed already, the first and primary responsibility of anyone who believes that they or their partner may have symptoms of autism is to get a proper evaluation and diagnosis. This is not the domain of a web questionnaire or even the informal opinion of your favorite family doctor; for an adult, it should be done by a psychiatrist or neurologist who specializes in autism spectrum disorders. The testing will likely be covered by your insurance if properly authorized in advance, although comprehensive reporting beyond a diagnosis may be elective and at your own cost.

> *The diagnosis was just the first step in unraveling the mystery of what made me tick in a way that would allow each of us to grow, change, adapt and accommodate the other.*

In my own case, after all the testing was complete, the doctor prepared the lengthy report already mentioned, detailing the results--some twenty pages of analysis, statistics, and graphs. My wife, Nicole, accompanied me to this meeting to receive the report, not only so that she could ask questions of the doctor but also so that we were receiving this information together, as a couple. I did not want it to be something I brought home from the doctor's office. Autism wasn't something that was newly inflicted upon our marriage simply because I now had a paper diagnosis. In fact, quite the contrary: the diagnosis was just the first step in unraveling the mystery of what made me tick in a way that would allow each of us -- not just me -- to grow, change, adapt and accommodate the other.

An autism diagnosis should never be looked at as an indictment or an excuse; it is neither. The symptoms of autism can certainly make any complex relationship more challenging, but they should never be used to explain away destructive or problematic behavior. Understanding the deeper origin of the symptoms does not exonerate the individual with autism from the effort needed to manage them or to protect the partner from the impact.

Similarly, just as the symptoms of autism are not to be used as an excuse, the individual who is affected by them should not be labeled or pigeonholed. A diagnosis is not a set of new limits imposed on the relationship: your path to happiness might have just become a lot more twisty, but the destination remains the same. And now you have a roadmap.

> *"I suspect there were a lot of 'Aha!' moments for my wife…"*

Likely the most critical aspect is that both partners accept the diagnosis. This starts the clock on improving two important aspects right away: the individual with autism may no longer feel crazy or broken, as though their idiosyncrasies are the cause of every malady in the relationship, while the neurotypical individual may go through an "Aha!" moment of "I told you something was up!" I'm on the wrong side of the equation to know for sure, but I suspect there were a *lot* of "Aha!" moments for my wife.

Most important, however, is how the diagnosis is used. It should not be used to place or excuse blame for anything, but as a roadmap to help you identify where the weakest spots in the relationship are so that you can work on them, regardless of where the ultimate responsibility may lie.

If the decision has been made to share the diagnosis with others, both the neurotypical and the individual with autism might benefit from the added support and advice of friends and relatives ... or this might truly complicate the situation. Use your best discretion.

## Understanding Autism for the Neurotypical

If you are the neurotypical partner in an autistic marriage, then reading this book is a good start. From here, however, you'll need to continue your education about autism to better understand the reality surrounding your marriage: a detailed understanding of autism can be a great help.

Several books are available that specifically address the challenges of the autistic marriage and of autism in general. If you are the partner of a high functioning person with the symptoms of autism you may also benefit from much of the material targeted towards Asperger's and marriage, as Asperger's was a much more common diagnosis in the years before the DSM psychiatric handbook was revised.

If you have been together as a couple for any length of time you likely understand your partner and their behavior very well already. You may even believe you can identify which aspects of their behavior are reflective of autism symptoms. However, unless you are a professional it would be hard to do so accurately, and unwise to try without the benefit of the most up-to-date research on autism. I encourage you to obtain as much information as possible from a variety of perspectives. Ask, read, and repeat!

# Understanding Autism for the Newly Diagnosed

When I first began to consider the implications of my own autism diagnosis, I was quite surprised to learn just how many of my behaviors appeared to be rooted in classic autism symptoms. What I did not realize, however, was just how many more there were: so many more than I had thought of before. In a few cases, I would be stunned to discover how deeply I was affected.

For example, I always knew that I had some difficulty with social situations, but I was entirely oblivious to my inability to correctly read others' emotions. It was only after my diagnosis that I would read and learn about mindblindness and stop to consider whether it applied to me. Once I had concluded that, indeed, I was somewhat blind to the inner emotional states of others, I could then come up with strategies to solve it, when possible, work around it at other times, or at least make others aware of the issue. This pattern repeated itself with numerous other autism features.

## Separating Can't from Won't

As the autistic half of a mixed relationship myself, I can only guess, but I imagine it must be incredibly frustrating to not truly, authoritatively know whether a troublesome behavior is one that the autistic partner *can't* change or one that they *won't* change. Are they using autism as an excuse for something they just don't want to work on? To do so would be, I believe, unconscionable. If the individual with autism is so tied to a characteristic that they refuse to change it, that refusal should be clearly made on principle on the grounds that it is fundamental to their persona, and not because it is a symptom of some named disorder and therefore to be excused as "not their fault." Almost anything can be defended, but never simply dismissed, ignored, or overlooked.

## Scheduling Time and Play

My wife and I met as teenagers, and in the small town in which we were growing up, the social options were limited and often amounted to going for coffee at a pancake house, donut shop, or similar. As mundane as this sounds, the hour of daily one-on-one, face-to-face social conversation -- particularly when it was just the two of us -- became a cornerstone of our early relationship that carried over into marriage. I also believe that years of these social over-coffee interactions and conversations were a formative training ground for me.

When I was writing software out of a tiny studio office as a teenager, Nicole would bring me lunch from Taco Time each and every day (people with autism do not like change); once married, when I was working and she was not yet, I would come home from Microsoft for lunch at our tiny apartment. Later, when we were both working, I would drive down and meet her for lunch by her office. Now that I am retired, we went for lunch most every day before the pandemic, and the hardest part is not growing too tired of the local restaurant menus!

This is really a dream scenario for an individual with autism such as me -- a loving relationship with a predictable, regular amount of interpersonal time spent directly communicating face to face for short windows of time each and almost every day. We came by this system not knowing any better, but it has served us as well as if it had been specifically prescribed for us. I believe regularly scheduled time between partners -- even if that means literally scheduling it on a whiteboard or calendar -- is essential. The individual with autism will certainly appreciate the predictability of it.

The neurotypical partner will not be surprised to learn that their partner with autism does not like change. To that end, sufficient advance notice of an interruption of these regular plans is critical. To the neurotypical, a last-minute change of plans that voids a lunch date might not be a big deal, but to the autistic partner who has anchored some of the structure of their day to it, such a material change at the last minute can be hard to accept. This does *not* mean you can't change plans on an autistic partner, or that said partner has a right to react poorly: it merely means that both parties recognize the impact on one person is very different than it might be on the other, and so each should try to accommodate this accordingly when possible.

Many couples that include a partner with autism must schedule their structures right down to their love life. Again, a predictable system that leaves less to chance might ruin the spark for some, but for others, it can be a huge boon to reducing stress and anxiety over the frequency of intimacy. Even sitting down to discuss the options can be elucidating, and you may learn a great deal about one another from the process of trying to negotiate an ideal schedule.

## Overloads and Meltdowns

Many individuals with autism experience meltdowns. Though hard to conceptualize for the neurotypical, a meltdown occurs when the amount of stress, strain, and stimulation the person with autism is exposed to exceeds their limits. They can range from merely actively withdrawing to a complete emotional breakdown with yelling, crying, and similar.

Meltdowns can be incredibly hard to manage in the moment for both partners, and each person is unique enough that managing a meltdown properly likely requires a personal approach tuned to their specific needs, insecurities, worries, and so on. It is much, much easier to avoid a meltdown than to manage one or to recover from it. Quite often, certain accommodations can be made for the autistic partner to reduce the load upon them, thereby reducing the chance of a meltdown in the first place.

Meltdowns deserve and receive attention in their own chapter.

## Making Accommodations for the Autistic Partner

The fact that a person has been diagnosed with autism does not automatically entitle them to a range of accommodations from the neurotypical partner. That said, however, accommodating the unique and special needs of the autistic partner when it is practical to do so just makes sense when a happy relationship is a goal for both people. It should not be viewed as a gift from the neurotypical, nor demanded as a right by the autistic -- it is simply the smartest and most effective way of managing the reality.

In my own case, one of the most problematic things to manage is the stress of travel. The combination of a lot of change all at once -- being out of your safe space, being out of control to a certain extent, alongside various other stressful factors -- all contribute to the overload. So much so that by the end of the first day of a particularly complex travel leg, about all I can do effectively is to relax and decompress. If pushed, for example, to go out for a big family dinner on the night of my arrival, I might not manage it well. It is just a poor recipe for success, something we've learned over the years.

However, it would not be a fair compromise to simply skip such obligations, because my wife loves family events. The solution in our case would be simply to move the dinner to a subsequent night, so I don't have to face it immediately after travel: everybody wins.

Accommodations are discussed in more detail in a later chapter.

## Compromises

It is inevitable that someone with autism is going to place at least a few unique demands upon a relationship, even if it is something as simple as needing time alone to themselves. A gregarious neurotypical partner may simply not be able to conceive of why the autistic partner might need time alone, in isolation, to decompress. They may view such a need as a rejection -- *Why on Earth would you spend time intentionally without me when we could be together?* -- but it is really nothing of the sort.

In my own life, although I love traveling with my entire family, it took us years of unknowing trial and error before we arrived at a workable system that allowed me to deviate somewhat from the itinerary of the rest of the (neurotypical) family. For example, as I write this chapter, I'm sitting in a quiet part of a darkened lounge on an enormous cruise ship off the coast of the Mexican Riviera, but the other seven family members are ashore enjoying the tropical sun. For whatever reason, the hot sun is not my thing, and I would not enjoy a full eight-hour day excursion of this sort, so I remained behind to write. Allowing for such a compromise wherein I skip a particularly "challenging" part of a family outing took many years; on such vacations my wife would feel guilty that I was left behind to "sit around with my laptop", and I would feel guilty that I was not actively participating with the family. Eventually, we realized that sometimes this is precisely what we *both* want, and it is OK to allow for it in limited doses!

That said, you can be certain that I have joined in on every other shore excursion on this trip -- from cooking some salsa to dancing the salsa. I have been snorkeling and sunbathing, visited the casino, shared every family dinner, spent time in the evening with everyone, taken my daughter for breakfast and my son for ice cream, played beer pong with the eldest, and so on. And therein lies the compromise: my wife's contribution is to allow for the fact that sometimes I truly am happier in a quiet place all by myself, while my own is to ensure that I am not there too long nor too often.

## Depression, Anxiety, OCD and ADD

As noted above, people with autism are also at a higher risk for depression, anxiety, OCD, and ADD. One of the primary complications for people with undiagnosed autism is severe, undiagnosed anxiety. Major anxiety can in turn cause a worsening of certain autism symptoms such as impulsivity, meltdowns, rage, and withdrawal -- all of which will have a significant negative impact on the marriage. This cyclic feedback loop can be very destructive to a relationship. The individual with autism experiences intense anxiety, perseverates, worries, and obsesses until they work themselves into a meltdown or panic attack, all of which not only damage the relationship but leave the individual with autism mentally drained, fragile, and prone to further meltdowns.

This merely underscores how important it is to get the autism diagnosis and then to begin managing any comorbid factors such as anxiety. It is critically important to diagnose and effectively treat depression, anxiety, OCD, or ADD/ADHD either with medications and/or counseling.

The load placed on the neurotypical partner can also lead to undiagnosed mental health issues, including anxiety, depression, affective deprivation disorder, and even post-traumatic stress disorder if living with an undiagnosed autistic partner has been sufficiently dramatic and stressful.

Problems with managing the anxiety of the individual with autism are common and can affect not only the relationship but the entire family. The individual with autism may, off on their own somewhere, become obsessively worried about something, come up with some protective solution in their head, and make a pronouncement of the "new way" things are going to be done to mitigate that risk without consulting anyone else. While driven by an urge to protect (or more accurately, perhaps to avoid unnecessary or unwanted change), it appears autocratic.

## Marriage Counseling and Motives

One of the secrets to a successful twenty-five-year marriage, if there are any, would be counseling when an issue becomes problematic. This is likely more important in a marriage involving someone on the autism spectrum. In my own case, I discovered late that I had been doing precisely what I have described with respect to mindblindness: assuming my wife feels and thinks exactly what I would think if I were in her position. It is, after all, sometimes all I have to go on! And therein lies a hint at the ultimate solution: more overt communication.

The worst thing you can do when arguing with someone with autism is to get into a "data debate" about who said what at what time, etc. Such arguments are rarely productive regardless of who the participants are, but when one party has an eidetic memory (or even merely believes they do) it can be pointless. I can be very hard to convince on subjective viewpoints, but if you simply tell me how you are *feeling*, it can make a huge difference. *That's* the piece I am usually missing, not the data.

Often, disputes in a marriage are always a layer or two below the surface. The partner who is upset about being ignored for too long at a cocktail party is likely seeking reassurance of their significance and importance, not a debate on how many minutes it technically was.

While there is a responsibility on the part of the neurotypical partner to communicate, or perhaps even over-communicate, the individual with autism bears the responsibility of not assuming motive on behalf of the other partner. In my own case at least, even though I believe myself to be only moderately impacted by mindblindness, I know that I am simply incapable of correctly inferring motive all the time. This is true even with the people I know the best. Since the cost of assuming an incorrect motive is high and can lead to conflict and hurt feelings, the onus is on the partner with autism to *ask* rather than to *assume* when it comes to motive. Far better to ask, "Why did you leave me to myself for an hour at the party?" than to assume it's because you're not important, get your feelings hurt, create an entire backstory around that in your own mind, and begin some obsessive perseveration over it! And of course, the neurotypical individual must resist the temptation to argue that "it was only forty-five minutes, not an hour." Presuming that the problem stems from an inability of the individual with autism to read the other person in some way, the solution will involve resolving the disconnect somehow and not denying its validity.

If the person with autism is to be convinced of anything, the effort should be on correcting the misconception about any *emotions* involved and not the *facts*. After all, they probably have a very good grasp of the facts, but a very sketchy view of the emotions tied to them––better to focus on the emotional implications of any particular scenario, helping them understand more fully what is in the minds of others.

## Welcome . . . to Fantasy Island!

In many very real ways, my wife has become my tour guide to a world of neurotypical interaction that was largely uninteresting to me, and hence, largely undiscovered as well. Take haggling over prices as an example: shortly after we were married, we went to Sears to buy a new refrigerator. Down in the basement of a dusty warehouse store my wife mercilessly haggled with the salesman on the price of the unit, even though it was already on sale -- and I didn't even know you *could* haggle at Sears! These games made no sense to me: I expected the lowest acceptable offer price to be listed on the tag already, but I've slowly learned how -- and more importantly when -- you can haggle on price. For example, it turns out that you can haggle on a refrigerator, but not a Denny's Grand Slam breakfast. Who knew?

Dealing with salespeople is but one tiny dimension of the bigger topic of dealing with people and with social situations, and that's where Nicole has been invaluable to me over the years as my sometimes-unwitting instructor.

For the first twenty-five years of marriage during which I was undiagnosed, when it came to dealing with other people, we just assumed that I was an introvert, and she was an extrovert; she would do outgoing things and I would do contemplative things. Over time I realized I was learning many new things from Nicole (and indeed, she from me as well), but I didn't realize I had effectively become her social protégé. Every outing for coffee, every dinner table conversation at her family's home, and every weekend outing with friends served as a training ground for me with her as my guide. More details about these early steps can be found in the chapter Making Friends with Autism.

## Masking

"You don't look autistic."

I get a lot of that. While I understand that it's generally well-meaning, it's hard not to take some offense as I wonder just what they imagine the alternatives to be. More than anything, however, I view it primarily as confirmation of just how authentic I've become in my masking.

Masking -- also known as camouflaging -- is the process of hiding one's internal feelings from the world and of putting on a "mask" of more "socially appropriate" emotions, actions, and feelings. It is putting on a disguise to appear essentially neurotypical so that a person with autism can fit in undetected amongst them. For example, if someone with autism symptoms that cause problems in social situations can manage them and hide any emotions and feelings from people around them, that is masking. People with autism who mask typically use internal "social scripts" that they have learned from others, often beginning as babies.

The reasons one might mask vary; some do it to connect better with their friends in a social environment. Others may mask to get a lucrative job, or even to pursue a romantic partner. In any situation where the person's natural response and reactions must be suppressed and a substitute, more acceptable and attractive façade placed on top, that is masking.

Even subtle modifications to your behavior could be considered masking. If you must brace your knee to avoid bouncing it or sit on your hands to avoid distracting others, that's masking -- and it might be wholly appropriate and considerate for the situation. And if, before a job interview, you must rehearse a few stories outside of your domain of interest and expertise, something that you can "perform" during the interview, that's also masking.

If your autism manifests itself in such a way as to give you something of a "flat affect" when you speak, then the enthusiasm and friendliness that you must muster to work in a retail sales job are masking too. If you work in customer service, over time you might develop an entire repertoire of "scenes" that you act out as the situation demands. "Returns? Absolutely! Right this way, sir!"

In my own case, one bit of feedback on my annual employee review suggested that a few new people on the team -- people who didn't know me well or at all even yet -- thought I was "grumpy." It turned out that only people who had not actually worked with me yet had that impression because operating at a distance, they had caught me not masking. People with autism don't always wear the facial expression you might expect. For example, I can be entirely content and happy but without a smile on my face, whereas almost all negative emotions tend to be conveyed via my expression as frustration or anger. Judging solely by my facial expression, I might appear to only ever be happy or annoyed to see you, and never in between, yet there may be numerous other emotions involved, just like you. In my case, they simply don't drive my expressions in the same automatic fashion, it seems.

The most basic goal of masking is simply to fit in with the crowd; to the extent that this is successful, it will increase the individual's chances of success in social relationships, employment, romance, and so on. Individuals with autism who are better able to hide or camouflage their symptoms will be able to make more neurotypical friends, improve their social support structures, and they will perform better in job interviews.

## Costs of Masking

Masking is not merely an effortless state that someone with autism can simply slip into. Even when well-practiced, masking is real intellectual work -- the most reported cost of masking is exhaustion, or even just simple mental fatigue from having to perform the masking for too long. I find that if I must be "ON" too long, I need a break -- if I am "on" for three to four hours, I need a half-hour or hour off, where I can decompress and not have to consider how every movement, word, moment of silence, or thought might be "wrong" for the situation. Quiet time, without social or interpersonal demands, is the remedy. The ratios will be different for each individual and will vary depending on the type of activity or interaction being performed.

Likely one of the worst cases for me is travel days, where I must travel all day across multiple connections and time zones to get to a remote destination like Saskatchewan, where I am then expected to entertain friends and relatives as soon as I arrive over a span of hours. Without a break in between the traveling and the entertaining, it's just too long of a run of masking. I simply cannot do it that long. For decades no one could understand why I needed a break upon arriving at my travel destination: it made no sense. What we were overlooking was the fact that I had been "working" on my performance all day already.

The more masking that a person with autism must do, the more draining it is, and enough masking can lower one's resilience to having a meltdown. A significant number of my own meltdowns have been related, it seems, to these long travel days that involve a great deal of masking. It lowers the stress reserves in some material way.

## You Mad, Dad?

A few neurotypical people -- many of whom I suspect are actually *somewhere* on the spectrum -- suffer from "grumpy resting face." The actress Anna Kendrick is a self-described sufferer of "resting bitch face", which now even has its own Wikipedia article. My father had a similar condition: he could be fully content, relaxed, and watching television, but when his face was at rest, particularly if he were thinking or concentrating, he often looked angry or annoyed. I cannot count the number of times as a child I nervously checked with him: "Dad -- what's wrong?" Each time I would measure the temperature and tone of his response as best I could to discern how genuine he was being when he said, "Nothing." Usually, however, he meant it, and I had been concerned only over a blank expression.

Knowing this had been an issue for me, long before I had any suspicions about autism whatsoever, I encouraged my own kids to ask as often as they wanted and reassured them up front that unless I had specifically *said* something, I likely wasn't mad. I also stressed that they could ask as often as they wanted. Since I'm not one of those people that would sulk around without having said anything, you're likely safe in the assurance that if I'm unhappy, it's rarely a secret, so just ask. Probably I wanted to avoid for my own kids some of the nervousness and angst I experienced in wondering about my own dad all the time.

This explicit exchange of courtesy reassurances doesn't really work in an office environment, however. My grumpy resting face wasn't an issue for people who knew me well, because my masking was refined enough that by the time you were actually interacting with me, I appeared normal and "happy." At a distance, or if you just watched me sitting in a meeting not speaking, perhaps, I most assuredly look grumpy and frustrated: but try to remember, it doesn't mean I am!

## Girls and Masking

Masking can hide the apparent symptoms of autism so effectively that it has also been blamed for delays in diagnosis, particularly among females. Perhaps girls are more adept at learning and/or emulating "normal" neurotypical traits and as such, they have a slightly higher likelihood of having undiagnosed symptoms of autism as a result. It is certainly a well-understood fact that males with autism are found in the general population at a rate of about four times that of females, but is it because their actual prevalence is that much higher or is some of it attributable to women being able to hide their diagnostic clues? And if so, what changes need to be made in the way we screen for and detect autism so that it does not preferentially detect or exclude autism in one gender over the other?

## The Ethics of Masking

Many people rightly push back on the very notion of masking at all: shouldn't we all be able to act ourselves, as individuals, and be accepted merely for who we are? Yes, that would be ideal. The reality is, however, that our society is not a heterogenous mixture of wildly different individuals. People in a society are in general far more alike than they are different, and it is these similarities that masking attempts to capitalize on.

In my own home, the approach I take is to be natural unless it's a special event (birthdays, Christmas, etc.) or we have company over. In those cases, I am expected to be "on", with all the aforementioned demands and time limits applied. Therefore, of course, I prefer to be natural. That does not mean rude, nor does it mean dismissive nor disinterested: when pressed to describe it one time, my family agreed on the adjective "factual."

I am sure there are many people, including some of my own friends and family, who would prefer that I be "on" at all times. Were it a simple decision and not an intellectually demanding performance, I might relent. In reality, however, I don't think that is possible nor fair.

Subject to the limitations of my own mindblindness, I know when it's needed most: when the new report card comes home, the new art is pinned to the fridge, after the performance in the play, and so on. In all these things, I am as genuinely excited and impressed internally as any parent would be, but I must specifically remember to express it openly lest it go unknown.

## Low Frustration Tolerance

We all prefer those times when things go our way; when the seas part and our path becomes clear and no barriers remain. In my own case, seeing anything operate like a well-oiled machine -- even an actual, well-oiled machine -- is very rewarding. Seeing anything complicate or frustrate its ability to operate is troubling to me: I immediately experience a form of anxiety and a compulsion to correct it. Imagine how much more troubling it must be when that which is frustrated is not some external machine but rather my own set of internal desires and expectations!

When things are not exactly as they should be, which is to say as I *want* them to be, it causes a level of anxiety, annoyance, and frustration that can far exceed that which neurotypical people experience. This may sound incredibly self-centered and self-focused, and indeed in some ways it undeniably is, but not in a toddler-wants-a-cookie manner. That is because low frustration tolerance does not stem from a belief that the person holds an esteemed position among others, but rather, from an intense internal belief that "things should be just so."

In other words, things should be as I wish them to be -- or at least as they usually are -- and I cannot stand it when they are not. Furthermore, things would be much better for everyone if they were generally always as they should be, and once I manage to set them so, others must not disturb them. Low frustration tolerance (LFT) is a very common feature of autism.

## It's (not Really) all about Me

Low frustration tolerance can appear at first a lot like unbridled narcissism, a belief that one's position in the universe is so special that things cannot, and must not, go wrong for them. It can seem as though we will only be happy if life is a never-ending parade of USB cables that plug in the right way the first time.

The LFT perspective is not that I must never be inconvenienced -- even I know that is unavoidable. That said, I do have the (not entirely reasonable) expectation that others won't needlessly cause me to encounter more frustration and annoyance than would be otherwise necessary. Put another way, the universe itself is arbitrary and capricious enough that I'd prefer you not to leave your car double-parked and blocking mine in because you'll "just be a few minutes." The feeling is almost one of: *We're all in this together, so let's make this as easy as possible for everyone involved.* When others do not play by the rules, and the result is a marked inconvenience, it feels very unnecessary and worse -- an injustice. People with autism are often very big on rules and justice, in part because both serve to make life a lot more predictable -- fewer changes.

## The Frustration of Intent

Frustration, anger, and intent are inextricably intertwined for me. Frustration can build towards anger, and that frustration can be sped along even more quickly when I believe that there is malicious or inconsiderate intent behind whatever insult or inconvenience is bothering me. Accidents are one thing, but intentionally hurting or inconveniencing me is another matter altogether, and it prompts a much higher level of frustration.

And *that* is why people on the spectrum must be extra careful. As discussed in the chapter on mindblindness, those with autism often suffer an inability to promptly and accurately determine the motives of those they interact with. The normal compensation is then to *assume* a motive, either as a logical deduction or as the only means of coming up with one, but it is quite often a shot in the dark that misses the mark. As noted earlier, one should "never attribute to malice that which can be sufficiently explained by incompetence." You would be well served to adopt a similar mantra in your daily business. This is particularly true with children, strangers, and others where your odds of guessing intent accurately are poor anyway. Incorrectly assuming intent is a major source of frustration.

## Improving Frustration Tolerance

My frustration tolerance has varied and does vary significantly based on my baseline mood and general level of contentment and optimism. Because of this, I am of the belief that anyone who wishes to do so must have at least *some* control over their frustration tolerance, even if it is not complete.

When I was a young man, before kids, my spouse and responsibilities came along, I seemed to have had the ability to dismiss many annoying situations with a simple "whatever." If something inconvenient or suboptimal were happening, and it did not impact me directly, I had by then acquired the ability to ignore things that were not relevant to me by simply saying, "Whatever... I didn't cause it, and it's no real hardship, so I have no responsibility to correct it." This simple tactic served me well until I had a wife and four kids to look after! Something changed internally at that point, and I lost that ability.

When a simple "doesn't matter" won't cut it, "doesn't affect me" is the next step up. If something that was right has been made wrong, but you can avoid the implications, take the opportunity to do so without becoming obsessed with the problem. When the urge to correct it arises, I remind myself that there is no direct win in improving things because the outcome does not impact me.

When the outcome *does* have an impact and is inconvenient, that's when the real fun begins. This is where an individual with autism must realize that, as mentioned earlier, they do not hold an esteemed position within the universe and are entitled to sail through life without complications. Plan for these possibilities--but how? First, the cost of any inconveniences can be reduced by allowing for buffers. Rather than leaving for the airport with just enough time remaining, build in an extra 30 minutes so that when something does go amiss, the costs are lower. You're only incurring a delay, not missing a flight, which is a significant difference. Delays are minor annoyances but missing a flight is a big deal.

If you are a neurotypical person traveling with someone on the spectrum, structure your schedule such that the inevitable delays and inconveniences that occur -- whether on vacation, a night out, or a trip to the grocery store -- do not rise to the level of causing significant stress.

# Accommodations

The basic philosophy for dealing with autism in any relationship that should emerge from these pages is one of compromise and shared responsibility. I believe the first and primary responsibility for accommodating one's needs and integrating oneself successfully into society falls on the self. After that, whatever they cannot do on their own they turn to others for assistance with. What remains, if anything, is a disability. The goal is not to eliminate the disorder, necessarily, nor even the symptoms, but to manage them in a way that prevents or minimizes the amount of disability.

In most cases, because I follow the do-it-yourself approach whenever possible, by the time accommodations are required, they may not be optional. In some cases, they might be needs, or realities.

## A Day at Disneyland

Is it a disability to not be able to march through Disneyland for a full eight-hour day followed by parades and fireworks at night without a break? It's not that I absolutely, positively, could *not* do it, but that when we did, it didn't work well. I suppose I knew I needed a break, but I sure didn't want to be the only Dad at Disneyland who needs a rest of this type. I'm fit and I work out and I'm not tired, so why would I need a rest or a break? And so, in the early years, I would tough it out and not take one, if for no other reason than simply that no one else around me needed one. In the rare cases I did, I felt quite bad for delaying the family's fun and for being perceived as out of shape, perhaps, or the odd one out.

At first, because what I had technically asked for was a rest or break, that's what Nicole attempted to arrange for me. We'd find a way to take a lunch or a picnic or some other *physical* rest break mid-day. But what she didn't understand (because I barely understood myself) was that it was not only a break from the activity that I needed: but instead, a break from *people*: all people, including loved ones, strangers, and cartoon actors. To neurotypical people, this can just seem weird.

Initially, it created some hurt feelings, I believe. First off, the family couldn't understand why I needed a break when no one else did. Moreover, why I did want to be away from them when they did not need to be away from me? That's hardly reciprocal. For years, then, we tried to operate as "normally" as possible, sometimes paying the price in frazzled nerves and the increased possibility of a meltdown when forced to operate all day without respite.

But what is it that I actually needed? Eventually, we settled on it: I would go back midday to the hotel on my own for an hour or two to "veg", as we would put it, then I'd be able to come back reenergized and ready for another half day at Disneyland. And so, once our income level could accommodate it, that's what we did: we started staying at the Grand Californian Hotel, which is next door to the park. We'd start at 8 am with a character breakfast, and then at about 1 pm, after lunch, I'd head from the park back to the hotel. I'd pull out my laptop, check my email, decompress, maybe watch a YouTube video, and have a little nap. Then about 2:30 pm I would head back and join the family at 3 pm and remain with them until dark. This approach makes me happy, and the family is happy, so it's a win all around. The alternative of just forcing myself through it could leave me emotionally sensitive and irritable, even in the happiest place on Earth. It took us *many* years to recognize and implement alternatives such as this across different styles of vacation, but we're much happier for having done so, and we travel much more successfully now.

This is but one of the many accommodations we have learned to make for autism. Our path was one of trial and error complicated by denial and a pervasive desire to be "normal," whatever that means. Once we got a handle on things and just started doing what worked, however, we were so much happier, and our travel became so much more successful. I can't overstate the importance of an outlook of shared responsibility. Although these accommodations were done for me, they were really approaches that we would implement together to make things better for all of us.

Of course, most of the accommodations that we have made for me were made long before we even knew that I had autism. We simply thought "Dave is just Dave," or "he's always been that way" and that I was "quirky," I guess--there were certain things I liked "just so." The primary difference now, post-diagnosis, is that I know I'm not entirely alone in these needs, and I feel slightly less odd in requesting certain accommodations.

## A Favorite Spot to Sit

As another example of accommodations that friends might make, one classic aspect of the character Sheldon on the television show *The Big Bang Theory* is that he has a particular place that he prefers to sit, and he acts as though it is a significant hardship for him to sit anywhere else. When pressed, he carefully explains the reasons for his selection:

- In the winter, that seat is close enough to the radiator to remain warm, but not so close as to cause perspiration.
- In the summer, it is directly in the path of a nice cross breeze because it is ideally located between three windows.
- The angle with which it faces the television is not so direct as to discourage conversation yet not so wide as to cause a parallax distortion in the view.
- And so on …

You might think Sheldon likes to sit in the same place all the time merely because people on the spectrum often work so hard to avoid change, but Sheldon's reluctance to move to another spot is not territorial or simply petty based on habit. He has invested a great deal of mental energy into determining the best spot to sit, and he does not want to needlessly lose those benefits without good cause. He would be painfully aware of every moment spent sitting in a less optimal spot. In other words, the moment he is forced to sit elsewhere all he can think of is the improper temperature, lack of a breeze, bad angle to the television, and so on … all of which could have been avoided if only they had listened to simple reason!

Even more frustrating* would be for Sheldon to lose his spot and to have said spot not put to good use by someone because they failed to appreciate the subtle benefits. If someone could make better use of it, he might gladly give it up, but it can feel like a big deal for such things to go to waste. If the spot is available, and it's very important to me and a trivial matter for others to accommodate, why not?

I, too, have a favorite spot to sit on my sofa and have many good reasons as to why it's the optimal spot for me. In fact, I wrote significant portions of this book sitting in it. In discussing this topic with my wife, I also learned that her parents (my in-laws) had accommodated me in a similar fashion by letting me have the same spot in their own home--and there I was thinking it was just conveniently always free! This is a prime example of an accommodation that those close to me had learned to make for me without knowing why. It's not that I'd ever ask someone to move if they took my spot, it's just that they normally do save it for me.

## Group Size

For me, the demand created by a social event is not tied directly to how many people are there, but more by how much masking I must do and how much I need to be "on" and present in a personal sense. For example, if I am hosting a gathering, I

---

* In this episode they effectively push Sheldon as far as they can until he ultimately can bend no further and he has a television version of a meltdown -- strained facial expressions and an inability to speak.

schedule it for three hours. My wife might prefer a five-hour come-and-go schedule for her own events, however. Five hours of continuous socializing is a wonderful day for her but would be more of a load for me than I would enjoy.

For others on the spectrum, the group size does matter as the social demands seem to go up linearly with however many people there are to meet, greet, get to know, and entertain.

## Staying on Schedule

People with autism like to know what's going to happen in advance. If planning an event that includes people on the spectrum, you will almost always be further ahead with a crisp schedule that is highly visual and that you stick to. If changes are needed, let them be known in advance with as much warning (i.e., time to mentally adjust to the changes) as possible.

*Our family schedule — color coded and highly visual for my benefit*

## Spontaneity

You might imagine that given the way people with autism usually resist change and how they can react badly to schedule interruptions, spontaneity would be a problem, and for many, it often is. Operating absent a prior plan, in an unknown environment, can be stressful and taxing emotionally.

I am OK with spontaneous plans if I still have some way that allows me to either demur entirely or to suggest an alternate plan that will better accommodate my needs or abilities. Metaphorically, I don't like being taken along for the ride, but I don't mind following as long as I get to drive my own car.

Let's say a group of friends suddenly decides to go for a movie and dinner. I might very well do only one or the other because to do both back-to-back might be too much. I don't find silently watching movies in the dark with other people to be a very social undertaking in the first place, so I'd likely attend just the dinner. It's not that I'm antisocial, it's just sometimes the plans are too much.

Don't be surprised, however, if your loved one on the spectrum is a little shy about spontaneous plans. The more detail you can provide in the mental picture of what to expect and in the scheduling overview, the easier it will make it for the person to participate.

## Quiet Time and Space

Perhaps the most fundamental accommodation for someone with autism is to give them the time and space in which to be themselves and where they can recover from social demands. When the need arises, there's some way to get a respite from the demands and distractions of whatever the social event is, be it a large party or simply regular family life.

Earplugs and noise-canceling headphones are helpful, but during larger events I've been known to disappear for twenty to thirty minutes and retreat to my master bedroom suite where I can hide out for a little bit, recharging and recuperating so that I can return to entertaining. I encourage you to do the same if needed -- just don't fall asleep!

## Asking for Accommodations

I recommend that you avoid being vague with statements such as "I have autism and it causes poor social skills," lest people think you simply have bad manners or a subpar personality! Be specific, saying things like "Because of my autism I'm not as good with verbal instructions and a written list that I can see is usually much more successful for me." Define the problem in terms of the specific accommodation you are seeking and not in a defect-first manner.

Accommodations need not be anything to be ashamed of. For example, when I was a young man, I first began to speak to my grandfather at length about his experiences in World War II, which began on the beaches of Normandy. I would learn that he was a much better communicator in person, likely because of significant hearing loss he'd developed in the Sherman Tanks he had ridden across Europe: he needed to read lips to compensate for that hearing deficiency. Unfortunately, I now lived a thousand miles away, so the telephone was our only line of communication at the time. His inability to hear me properly meant that our conversations were short and unsatisfying.

Then one day he called me with his newly received hearing aids in. They were transformational, and our first conversation went on for what seemed like hours. It flowed with ease like never before. It was almost like being able to speak with someone who had been largely mute until then. The stories poured forth as I peppered him with question after question. When the call finally ended, I had that rare feeling of having just discovered a great new untapped resource. Sadly, he would pass not long after that; our one epic conversation would turn out to be our only one like it, but it's an experience that I still treasure today.

His hearing aids were an accommodation of the reality that he simply could not communicate well without them. If you are reading this as a person with autism and have features that cause pathological symptoms, and those symptoms can be avoided or at least mitigated by reasonable accommodations, I recommend looking at them in a similar fashion: simple changes that work to the benefit of everyone involved.

## Meltdowns

A meltdown occurs when an individual with autism[*] temporarily loses the ability to adequately control emotional responses to either external (often environmental) factors, or to internal emotional ones. This results in a catastrophic reaction as the individual loses control and the upset boils over. Meltdowns generally go in one of two directions: internalized and externalized. When internalized the meltdown may be

---

[*] Meltdowns have also been reported, though far less commonly, in individuals with Sensory Processing Disorders and Attention Deficit Disorder.

accompanied by intense self-hatred, blame, and depression--even rising to the level of suicidal thoughts or thoughts of harm. When externalized, for some it can even manifest in aggression or property destruction.

Before I knew that I had autism, I thought my own meltdowns were panic attacks. My primary response would be to retreat to my room and to block out as much light and sound as possible; reducing stimuli was often key. And yet, at least in most of my own examples, the primary emotion was never simply one of panic. Certainly, fear was the primary component, but it was not a fear of what was happening or what had happened so much as an intense frustration that the current status quo was a new normal that I could not accept, and therefore I had to somehow will it or argue it away. We know the fear of change is a critical emotion in people with autism, and too much of it can certainly lead to a meltdown.

On the surface, a meltdown may seem like a panic attack or even a temper tantrum but they are very different both in their triggers and in how they are experienced. When a neurotypical child is having a temper tantrum, giving in to the demand will resolve the tantrum: a child crying over candy will stop crying when given candy. With a meltdown, the removal of the original stimulus does not resolve the problem. A meltdown is an outcome, not a tactic employed by autistic children to get their way (which is not to say that a clever child could not intentionally exploit meltdowns, but merely that they will occur naturally regardless).

That said, a meltdown could serve as inadvertent communication to others around. I know of one teenager on the spectrum who placed a favorite chicken in a relative's care. Unfortunately, the chicken was subsequently killed by dogs. The chicken owner with autism was apoplectic for reasons no one could quite understand -- *How close could a person really be to a chicken?* But perhaps that was exactly the point, though almost certainly not intentional: if the teen were to try to articulate the depth of their rage/angst/mourning over the chicken in words or stories, no one would likely understand. Being that attached to a chicken likely wouldn't make sense to them anyway. But in the throes of a meltdown, it becomes amply clear to everyone around just how important the chicken was to the teen. The "why" will remain elusive, and "what to do" is not furthered at all, but there can be no confusion over the level of importance the chicken has to the teenager. I do not mean this to imply that people with autism experience meltdowns as mechanisms for intentionally communicating their depth of upset, merely that they may accidentally serve as clues for those around them when more sophisticated means of communication escape the individual with autism in the moment.

Another individual, self-described as "high functioning," reported the sudden and intense desire to destroy a batch of their recently completed fine carpentry during a meltdown. The motivation (never acted upon) was not one of wanton destruction, and the meltdown was unrelated to the woodwork. It was instead a flailing attempt at communicating to those around him of just how deeply disturbing the meltdown experience was. Hypothetically speaking, destroying their work would demonstrate a level of upset akin to the level of upset experienced during the meltdown. The impulse to act out came from a desire to express how deeply disturbed they felt, it was not about retribution or destruction.

Having a favorite chicken taken violently is one thing; not being able to get breaded chicken in the precise flavor or shape that a child is used to is another. But the latter can cause enough upset to precipitate a meltdown in a child who is sensitive enough to change. A child who enjoys a favorite restaurant on Wednesdays may have a meltdown if, for example, the dining area is closed for renovations and only take-out is available. The food is the same, but the experience is different, and this may set the child into the early stages of a meltdown. Although triggered initially by intense dissatisfaction with the situation, there's no way in which the meltdown can be manipulative (as with a temper tantrum) since both the child and the parent know the dining area will not magically open no matter how much angst results.

Many people with autism will experience meltdowns at inopportune times: some frequently, some very rarely. The goal in all cases should be to reduce the frequency, severity, impact, and duration of the meltdowns. In my own case, the frequency of meltdowns tracks rather closely the overall level of my mental resilience. If I am in the midst of stressful travel, a meltdown is much more likely than if I am at home in my safe, comfortable, and regular space.

I do not have many regrets stemming from my autism, but if there is one, it is having had my children witness their father amid a meltdown. My own episodes are rare but allow me to be candid -- it's more-than-somewhat inconvenient and embarrassing for a grown person to break down and cry or rage over accumulated frustration or annoyance, no matter what the cause. So, they're still not rare enough -- "never" would be ideal for me.

My solution to handling a meltdown is to remove myself from the situation and then to remove as much stimulus as I can. For me, this literally means going to my darkened room, laying on the bed, donning noise-canceling headphones, and placing a pillow over my eyes such that I am largely insulated from the world. Then I self-soothe, meditate, and wait. Most times it will have largely passed in twenty or thirty minutes, but not always.

After years of trial and error, my wife knows that this is a recovery process and can only be accelerated so much. She'll check on me -- perhaps at the ten-minute mark--and then every fifteen to twenty minutes later, perhaps offering some encouragement (but it's hard to know what to say, I'm sure) or merely letting me know that she's there and on my side when I'm ready.

During this period the biggest mental challenge for me is not to "catastrophize" events. I'm sure every person is different, but for me, it becomes very easy to get stuck on the thought cycle of "*this is a new normal, and it causes me a great deal of angst, and now this new normal is apparently permanent, and there's nothing I can do but live with it, and I don't know how to live with it.*" This assessment is very rarely accurate, of course, but I will obsess and dwell on it endlessly if not careful.

A meltdown is a painful emotional experience, one that the individual would desperately like to escape, and thus during a meltdown, the fight-or-flight instinct is highly triggered. In an individual who lacks aggression (or when it is fully controlled), sufficient overstimulation means that only flight remains. The compulsion to leave the situation -- which can be helpful or injurious depending entirely on circumstances -- can be overwhelming.

Every person is different, but many other individuals with autism also report needing to withdraw to a safe space to recover, which can take time: minutes or hours. After a meltdown, the person typically feels ashamed, embarrassed, physically drained, and mentally exhausted, and they will experience a "mental hangover" feeling that can persist for days. They may even withdraw for a day to rest and recuperate.

I tend to remember very little of what was going on inside my head during the worst of it. Within a couple of days, I will largely have a void in my memory which is where the meltdown took place. I will remember the events that precipitated it and that followed it, but little from the midst of it beyond the important highlights.

## Having a Meltdown is neither a Failure nor a Choice

In the moment it can be difficult not to do this, but it's important not to judge the person having the meltdown -- after all, for whatever reasons, they are now (by definition) operating outside the scope of their abilities, out in unknown territory. A meltdown is not a chosen response to a situation; it is at least as unwanted by the individual with autism as it is by those who surround them.

Managing a meltdown must be tailored to the individual and their abilities. The general steps to managing a meltdown are:

- Give the person some time and space. To the extent that is practical, try to accommodate their need to reduce stimulus and input as much as possible: a quiet, darkened room might be ideal, a rolled towel across the eyes can be used to limit light.
- Check back periodically to see if they are ready to discuss or be comforted, perhaps every 5 to 15 minutes. The interval depends on the individual and the situation.
- If they wish to argue, don't engage or dismiss, just delay. There is little practical purpose in debating or arguing any details or data.
- When it seems like it might finally be productive to do so, calmly inquire as to what is the fundamental source of the overwhelming emotional state. If the primary goal is to calm the meltdown, the most important fact to ascertain is the *why* and to offer whatever assurances can be given against the dreaded outcome, whatever that is.
- A person with very significant autism symptoms might have a meltdown due to the noise from fluorescent lights or loud music. In those cases, reducing the noise volume is the first step. If the source of the reaction is rooted in insecurity over some personal slight -- real or imagined -- then the best tactic is to offer reassurance and affirmation around it without debating the details.

If you are the neurotypical person in a mixed relationship, and you've been through all this before, then you've no doubt periodically wondered why it is your responsibility at all to help a grown adult through what essentially looks like a giant temper tantrum? *Won't they simply "grow out of it" at some point?*

Unfortunately, while they can certainly improve and become more resilient, there will *always* be a point at which a person with autism's mind becomes overloaded, spinning down into conflict mode. A meltdown isn't something a person with autism does, but rather, something they *fail* to do: meltdowns occur when the individual fails to adequately cope with the amount of emotional and psychic input being delivered over some window of time. They do not have a choice at that point. Even though they are certainly responsible for their actions while in such a state, the question then becomes whether the individual with autism is culpable for entering that state, and that is much harder to know.

There is no value to be had in a meltdown; I would never choose to have one, nor allow myself to slip into one if I could in any way avoid it. I appear angry, I am less articulate, less likely to convince, and less likely to get the actual outcome I prefer or need. They are embarrassing, damaging to relationships, frighten children, take time to recover from, and weaken my resilience toward future episodes. Until I was diagnosed, I did not actually even know what an autistic meltdown was, nor that I was having them. They simply did not and could not register with me as meltdowns because I had never even heard the term -- I presumed I had been having panic attacks of some sort. Lacking a better name, Nicole and I referred to them as "episodes."

## The Rumble Stage

Meltdowns do not happen in a vacuum; they are almost always precipitated by a long or severe series of stressors that upset or frustrate the individual with autism. Perhaps the most maddening scenario for a particularly smart individual with autism is to be right but entirely frustrated in their efforts -- when others in positions of power over them are frustrating their (self-perceived) virtuous efforts or desires. If the matter at hand is sufficiently important, I can think of no better way to precipitate a meltdown.

In my own case, I believe I enter a "rumble stage" wherein the meltdown becomes increasingly likely but is still avoidable. I will begin to seek reassurance or investigate the overall scenario for evidence of a motive--because if I hypothesize one that I do not like, I will perseverate over it intensely. I might begin to get restless or even pace. Others might rock or rub their legs. If it's possible to feel sorry for myself over the issue, or if it causes me a great deal of anxiety over an injustice, then it can be enough to form the perfect storm that will launch a meltdown.

## Neurofeedback and Meditation

Distraction, diversion, reassurance, and calming strategies may all contribute to avoiding a meltdown during the rumble stage. I also believe that neurofeedback training has helped me control my brain state such that it makes me less likely these days to enter the meltdown state. Over time I am becoming somewhat adept at catching these runaway trains, but it's an effort that must be consciously exerted and repeatedly practiced.

I began neurofeedback training to see whether I would receive any positive benefits for my ADD and focus issues. The notion that it might be useful for autism was far from my mind and indeed, even seemed a little offensive to me (I wasn't eager to be "fixed", after all). The training sessions, as far as I knew, were intended strictly for my ADD issues.

The training that I have undertaken uses a multi-channel "brain wave detector array" connected to a computer that reads the "state" of my active brain. While the scanner is monitoring my mind, I watch a movie. The picture that I see is modified by the computer-based on how well I am paying attention. If I am not doing the right things -- by its rules -- then the picture will become smaller, further away, more washed out in color, and the audio will become flat and hushed. If I pay "correct" attention to the video, however, the brain scanner will notice it and so instruct the computer to "reward" me by improving the picture quality, returning the image to one that is bright, clear, large, and vivid. Each session of the training runs for an hour and is repeated a couple of times a week for weeks on end. By the end of a couple of months, I was certain that I could command that brain state at will, although the doctor was a tad more skeptical: she felt that only classically trained yogis could typically do it so quickly.

It wasn't quite *that* simple, but it was true indeed: if I encountered stress that was starting to disturb me, I found that if I sat quietly and made the effort, I could get my brain to enter what I am confident to be the same relaxed and open-minded state as during the neurofeedback training. I have little to no experience with eastern meditation, but I expect that similar results -- and a similar ability to relax on command -- might be achievable for many.

Soon, I would attempt to apply this newfound skill to my autism. When I felt the rumble stage of a meltdown coming on, I would move to a quiet room where I could attempt to get my brain into a special relaxed state. Almost every time I made such an effort, I was successful.

In fact, I was able to avoid meltdowns entirely for a very long time if I was able to catch myself and intentionally make the effort to avoid one. The only times I would fail, I found, were if I were in a time and/or place that made it impossible or impractical for me to get the required amount of isolation and quiet needed, or if I simply failed by not choosing soon enough. Being out of practice seemed to matter as well. It's not a permanent change, it seems, but a skill that, like a language, must be used to be maintained.

I found this notion of making the resolution to not have a meltdown early in the process to be important -- left too long, you'll convince yourself of the self-righteous nature of whatever is agitating you. To use a flight analogy, you can't wait until you've already hit the ground to pull back on the stick. You must apply all your efforts as early into the process as possible for maximum success.

# Anger

Anger can be a real problem with autism. It's also an area where I worry that people with autism might have a large blind spot about themselves: the anger that accompanies autism often has a self-righteous, logical, justified feel to it, in the sense that *if the world would just take my advice, things would be OK*. In that sense, the anger can feel justified -- after all, reality *did* fail to comply with my wishes. That feeling of justification can impair the individual's ability to see how the consequences of their anger can impact those around them.

It seems with autism that at times the frustrations of life can accelerate the anger response more quickly than the mind can rein it back in. The neurotypical response that mutes or combats anger seems impaired in some way. As a result, anger can rise too quickly, and the speed and intensity with which anger accumulates can be extreme -- much faster than the individual with autism can compensate for or react to.

When someone with autism is stimulated in a way that causes anger, they do not appear to be able to pause or consider alternate strategies for resolving the situation -- the first response when someone attempts to redirect them from their anger seems to be to "double-down" on the original one as if to ensure it is not overlooked, which in turn increases the intensity of the response.

Since individuals with ASD may experience significant irritability and low frustration tolerance, they may cycle from calm to angry in a very short time. This short window further complicates the fact that they may lack de-escalation skills that help them catch and calm themselves along the way.

Just as frustration can lead to a meltdown, however, unchecked anger can rise to a rage -- and just as meltdowns have a rumble stage, so does rage.

## Anger's Rumble Stage

As anger builds within the individual, expressions of it will begin to emerge:

- Fidgeting, chewing, tapping, etc.
- Stimming behaviors
- Repetitive behaviors
- Vocalizations and mumbling
- Swearing, profanity, complaints
- Increases in movement
- Walking in circles and pacing
- Leaving the room or house to escape

## Rage

Anger that builds unchecked will eventually rise to the level of a rage. Like a meltdown, the individual has lost control, but rather than frustration and hopelessness, anger is the overarching emotion.

Legally, ethically, and morally, the person is still wholly culpable for their actions, but the individual has lost practical control over themselves:

- The individual loses control mentally and physically
- Noise and destruction

- Screaming
- Explosive impulses
- Biting, hitting, kicking
- Destruction of property
- Injury of Self
- Injury of Others

## Recovery

Following a rage, a recovery period ensues during which the brain recovers. Typically:

- Crying
- Apologizing
- Minimization of impact as though nothing had happened

If the anger and rage have begun to move into the pathological realm, which may include precursors to abuse, then other characteristics may rise to the surface:

- Denial of rage
- Shifting of blame
- Pleas to never repeat
- Gift giving to compensate
- Inappropriate smiling or facial expressions

## Jekyll and Hyde Syndrome

How can it be that someone with high function autism symptoms can function and control their emotions and negative behaviors in a professional capacity but not a personal one? In my own case I didn't seem to have a distinction -- the challenges I faced at work, particularly when it was my own company -- were as emotionally demanding and as personal as those at home. For others, particularly professionals such as doctors and judges that must maintain a particular façade however, I suspect that they maintain almost two fronts or personalities, and that home is believed to be a place of refuge and sanctuary. Perhaps they absorb and store the stressors of the day in an ineffective way, but whatever the cause, it is sometimes released upon the home when they arrive, and rarely in a welcome manner.

Just as everyone is different, each manifestation of ASD will be different, and the anger dimension must be included in that. I certainly have struggled with anger in my own experience, but it has never escalated past leaving the scene. On two or three occasions in my life, when I felt that I was approaching the horizon of where I could see the loss of control, I have gone for a walk or disappeared to complete some other pointless errand. For better and worse, this gave me time, space, and distance in which to decompress.

## Domestic Abuse

The decision to commit an act of abuse is unrelated to a person's placement on the spectrum. While people with ASD face anger and even rage challenges that surpass those that neurotypical individuals face, abuse does not come from a place of anger but of control. I see no reason to claim or suspect that domestic violence is any more prevalent in homes where ASD presents a challenge -- and the studies I was able to locate showed no indication that ASD leads to higher rates of domestic abuse -- in fact, statistically, those with ASD are more likely to be the victims of abuse.

If ASD can in some cases lead to out-of-control rages, however, you might wonder how abuse is not rampant. As mentioned, I believe that is because abuse is an extension of control, not anger. ASD homes might be struggling frequently with bouts of anger and even rage that never escalates to violence. Even the most intense rages can lack any characteristics of physical abuse. But why? How?

My belief is that most actual abusers are not, in fact, "out of control" at all. They seem to control themselves quite well until no one else is around to see their abusive behavior. They are able to stop their abuse when it is to their advantage to do so, such as when the police or their boss shows up. Violent abusers plan their blows so as to land where they will be less visible. They pick and choose who to abuse and distribute their wrath unevenly. None of this has anything to do with autistic behavior.

Figuring out how that anger is managed, channeled, deflected, and diffused can be a lifetime challenge for the individual with ASD, but it need never be conflated with abusive behavior unless and until it takes on its characteristics. If and when it does, outside help should be sought immediately. As always, if it constitutes an emergency or if you witness or suspect domestic abuse, contact 911.

I imagine there are many families with children that have autism where the child has demonstrated a prior tendency towards becoming aggressive towards or even hitting the parent during a meltdown. This is a behavior that must be modulated and controlled before the child grows to a size where he or she will be able to overpower or injure the responsible adult. I recommend promptly investigating counseling and therapy from an expert who can provide advice specific to your family's situation.

## Anger Management and Behavior Therapy

In relationships that are free from any abusive behaviors but where anger and rage have still played a prominent role, the impact on loved ones can be significant. Because the anger is usually a result of the emotional state of the individual with autism and not the result of any act that they themselves committed, those around them feel as though they never know when the anger will be triggered. Loved ones can come to feel as though they are "walking on eggshells" around their partner. Left unchecked, it is possible that this could lead to resentment over time.

As discussed in the chapter on meltdowns, I believe that I derived benefit from the neurofeedback sessions I was undergoing. The goal had been to help with issues related to my attention deficit disorder, but I found that the brain state of being focused was also calming. As I became more adept at managing my focus, I found this new ability to settle my brain state quite helpful in catching any anger before it ran away. If anything approached the rumble stage, I could take a break and meditate, often effectively stemming any further escalation of my mood and allowing a return to a calmer state.

If anger becomes a problem for you or your family, or if it ever rises to the level of a rage, regardless of how well it is managed, I strongly recommend prompt professional advice. While traditional anger management and cognitive behavioral therapy likely offer significant benefits, finding a provider who is intimately familiar with the anger issues surrounding autism is always preferred.

## Making Friends with Autism

Making friends when you have autism can sometimes be difficult. The numerous social deficits that can encumber those with autism symptoms begin to manifest as soon as a person enters a social environment, and for many today, that will be preschool or kindergarten. While these early days are often spent forming lasting friendships amongst the neurotypical, the kids with autism must fumble their way through the process, grasping for handholds and looking for clues, as none of it seems to come naturally for them. Not only do they lack the natural ability, but in many cases, they also lack the drive or impetus to *be* social in the first place.

Why is it often difficult for the autistic to form new friendships? The following are but a few potential reasons.

- Limited focus of interest – the autistic child may be highly focused on one topic (such as dinosaurs) to the exclusion of almost everything else which limits play appeal with other children.
- Lack of reciprocal interest. People love to be heard and the autistic child may spend much more time talking/showing than listening to the other children.
- Difficulty reading non-verbal social cues and nuances in language and tone leads to misunderstandings.

- Trouble seeing things from another's perspective can cause conflict.
- Eye contact can be difficult or labored.
- Perception of the person with autism as aloof, cold, standoffish, etc.
- Certain behaviors can be "annoying" to the neurotypical.

Taken all together, these factors can make it challenging to make a good first impression! I have found consistently that most of my friendships (and courtships) were built over time: it takes a long while to "get me" and to get to know me. There have been numerous times in my life when friends, coworkers, and acquaintances, who have known me perhaps a few months, have marveled at how mistaken they were in their first assessment or impression of me. This is something I've undertaken to address since my diagnosis.

In my experience, those with autism tend to have one or two very close friends rather than large groups of acquaintances. Their closest friends will often be neurotypical: think Kirk and Spock, not Butch and Cassidy.

> *Children with autism often describe their experience with other children as being 'tolerated' rather than fully included.*

Kids with autism mature at a different rate -- often faster intellectually but generally more slowly socially and in terms of maturity level. This can push them to the periphery of the playground where they then -- either by choice or necessity -- often remain. When they try to get involved with the neurotypical children, their attempts can be seen as immature and might even be perceived as annoying or irritating by other children, who wind up rejecting the child with autism until they slowly adapt their behavior -- if indeed they ever do -- to better fit in with the social norms. Children with autism often describe their experience with other children as being "tolerated" rather than fully included.

Generalizations are dangerous, but with that risk in mind, many people with autism are not gregarious and typically do not derive a great deal of pleasure from the process of going out and meeting large numbers of new people. Thus, not only is the pool of people from which friends can be drawn smaller but, in many cases, the individual with autism is simply less adept at the social practices used to meet new people and to establish the early parts of any relationship or friendship.

Masking oneself for too long -- or too often -- can lead to a surreal feeling where the person with autism feels like they don't even know who they are anymore: they've been "faking it" for so long that they've developed an entire external persona of which to keep track. It can also be hard on one's self-esteem to realize that your own personality, actions, and feelings are not acceptable to the world and must be hidden or suppressed.

# How Not to Win Friends or Influence People

Dale Carnegie's famous book *How to Win Friends and Influence People* was by no means the first nor will it be the last words in social guidance, but it is a classic to be sure. It contains a useful and time-tested framework that we can turn to in order to study the mechanics of making and keeping friends. The birds-eye view of the book might be grossly summarized as follows:

- Do not criticize, condemn, complain, or point out faults.
- Give frequent and sincere appreciation.
- Smile frequently.
- Remember and use the person's name -- they love to hear it.
- Be a great listener, encouraging others to talk about themselves.
- Be *genuinely* interested in *other* people's interests and talk primarily about things of interest to *them*.
- Make the other person feel sincerely important.

> *"When dealing with people, let us remember we are not dealing with creatures of **logic** -- We are dealing with creatures of **emotion**..."*
>
> Dale Carnegie
> [Emphasis Added]

I cannot speak for anyone else on the spectrum, but this is a list of things that certainly did not come naturally to me. In fact, a lot of it sounds downright contrary to the nature of most of the people with autism that I know. That's neither through malice nor disinterest: for example, if something important is going on in your life, I absolutely want to know. If it's important to you, it's important to me. The difference is that I likely do not want to spend twenty minutes talking about travel, the weather, or the local sports team's latest contest if, in fact, there's nothing substantially new going on.

Thanks to decades of unplanned social training in hardware stores, barbershops, coffee shops, and around the dinner table, I've learned that Carnegie's strategies as enumerated above do indeed work! I mean that quite literally, however: it's taken decades for me to pick up habits and skills that, if they had been taught to me outright because I was at a known deficit, would have saved me many years of trial and a lot of errors.

## Working Outside Your Comfort Zone

When I first learned that I had I Autism, I felt somehow constrained and limited by the diagnosis. I wanted to push back in each way that I felt autism was limiting me, and so over the course of the next year or two, I undertook several initiatives intended to force me to operate "outside my comfort zone", which is where I've always believed that the most growth occurs. I started writing this book as but one example. I also hosted a large, catered, open-house party for dozens of friends and acquaintances at my workshop. The most challenging for me, however, was to start a YouTube* channel where I would broadcast myself to anyone willing to watch and listen. My subject matter was rather obscure -- programming topics, the history of Microsoft, and various projects that I'm working on. In addition to learning the technical side of video editing and production, I had to come to terms with editing my own smiling face in 4K resolution for hours at a time.

I believe the YouTube channel has been essential in developing my masking and communications skills, and even I can see a huge improvement over the course of the year or two that I've been doing it. My audience has grown slowly but steadily, eventually surpassing the 5,000 subscriber mark, then 25,000, then 100,000. With over 150,000 current subscribers, I write, record, edit, and produce about one video segment per week.

## Basic Skills

When Bill Gates was growing up, his mother clearly sensed that -- in a way not true of his siblings -- he needed a lot more practice in the social arena. She kept him very active doing things that I suspect were not easy for him, but that were likely huge growth and development opportunities. For example, he

---

* Dave's Garage, http://youtube.com/c/davesgarage

served as an usher or greeter at many of his father's business events, complete with a tuxedo. But even more challenging, perhaps, was the dinnertime tradition wherein the children were rotated amongst neighborhood homes for dinner at a new home each night for a week or more. Each child would have to eat what their hosts ate, follow their customs, and participate in their conversations.

I have no idea how much of this would have constituted "exposure therapy" to reduce anxiety over these types of events versus just practicing new skills and abilities, but at least had it been me, it would likely have served both purposes!

My own training was not so rigorous. Once out of high school I fell in with a close group of neurotypical guys. Kris, Chris, and Chuck might have appeared dangerous to my parents when dressed in their finest heavy metal concert tees, but the only laws that we broke were with our cars as we cruised aimlessly, street raced, hung out at the local park, and generally accomplished very little for a couple of years. What we did, however, was socialize: with each other, with new friends, with old friends, and with those few girls that were willing to talk to us. What I had once believed to have been a few "lost years" were really a crash course in normalcy sorely needed to help prepare me for love, marriage, and career. Without those guys, I would never have caught up in terms of the maturity and confidence needed to win Nicole's heart, and without *that*, none of the rest would have been possible.

## The Social Ladder

Oft times, when we speak of "climbing the social ladder", we mean the process of working your way up some real or imagined hierarchy of individuals, perhaps to get a better seat at the dining table. In this case, however, I mean ascending the ladder of social ability. I've used a ladder for the metaphor in this case because I believe each rung, or step up, provides the opportunity for an even higher handhold and further climbing.

For many autistic kids, the disappointment of social rejection might begin as early as preschool. And, while there is no convincing logical or objective argument as to why someone with autism should learn to act differently than their natural instincts might inform them to, the simple fact remains that unless the individual with autism makes a concerted effort to fit in, they likely will not be able to. As noted earlier, as individuals with autism our instincts, mannerisms, habits, and even our gestures, posture, and movements can be seen as "weird" and "different" by the neurotypical. Our fascination with a limited set of topics and general disinterest in the motives of others can be off-putting. Our general demeanor might be more reserved, making us harder to get to know at all. And yet, for all our lack of ability in this specific arena, and even in many cases our complete lack of desire for the process, we still *want* to have close friends as much as anyone does, even if we're not the best at making them.

## Growing Your Skills

If you will grant that improving your odds of success in the many realms affected by social interaction is a worthy pursuit, then it stands to reason that a roadmap of sorts would be helpful. To that end, we return to Carnegie's work for the broad strokes of what he believed to be most important in dealing with other people.

## Correcting Others

One of the first serious talks I had to have with my second-born was about his propensity for correcting people. One of the wisest and most precocious children I've ever had the pleasure of knowing, he was openly challenging his science teachers -- and often winning -- before he was ten years old. As with most things, however, sometimes discretion is the better part of valor. Even if a debt is owed to the truth, I told him, perhaps it can be collected in private, rather than embarrassing the person you need to correct in front of an audience. And yet, I didn't want to do anything to discourage his inquisitiveness or willingness to challenge authority when appropriate. *What to do?*

To make it his decision, I opted to stress the importance of the cost tradeoff. Every time you correct someone--even in private, there is a cost. It might create an air of distrust or insecurity, or even worse. The best case still likely involves a slightly bruised ego at a minimum. Whatever the case, the costs are never truly zero. Try to understand what they might be before you act.

The question, then, is more sophisticated than merely "should I say something?" The question really becomes: "What is the tradeoff I invoke by doing so?" If you are responsible for the Space Shuttle's rubber O-rings on the morning of a freezing cold launch, then you absolutely **must** speak up. But perhaps not every inconsequential vocabulary error that someone commits in front of you needs to be pointed out. If you are truly applying discretion to consciously deciding what's worth correcting -- and not merely reacting on instinct -- you should be fine.

## Disagreeing with Others

*How* you disagree with someone can be as important as *whether* you do so in the first place. When a factual misstatement is made that someone with autism is present for, it can create a sense of "pressure" that drives them to offer a correction. This drive is not about showing the other person up, however, nor even is it a show of knowledge: it is more about correcting the record for the sake of the truth and accuracy. Moreover, it is not about making them intentionally feel bad or embarrassed about their mistake, and you would be well served, then, to make sure you do not do so inadvertently either.

If this is indeed an instance where it is worthwhile offering the correction, always try to do it in a way that (a) allows the mistaken party to save face, and (b) makes it clear that the goal is to get the right info, not to make them look bad publicly.

## Trivial Information

Imagine you are waiting in line for It's a Small World* at Disneyland when you strike up a conversation with the stranger in line next to you. During the discussion, they

---

* A children's attraction with a notoriously repetitive, but infectiously cheerful, theme song.

casually mention that they grew up in Hometown, PA, which just also happens to be *your* original hometown as well! The feeling of "you're kidding, I'm from there too!" is very similar to the feeling that I experience when any piece of trivial, tangential information rises to the surface. Not only does it feel important to share, but it might also feel odd if it comes up later and you hadn't mentioned it now, because it's so topical to the current discussion. Whether it's a relevant piece of scientific trivia or a reference to an episode of *The Simpsons*, people with autism often feel compelled to share related information in a similar way. It's the same pressure that a neurotypical person might feel to share an important emotional or interpersonal detail.

The difference can be found in the symmetry of interest. In the hometown case, *both* parties will have a similar level of interest and fascination with the fact, so it makes sense to share it between them. In the case of a piece of other trivia bubbling up to the surface, it might only be a source of fascination to the speaker, and hence, ultimately annoying and distracting to other people. A person with autism should consider carefully whether sharing it will benefit and/or entertain the audience. If relating the information will serve as just a release for themselves, better to abstain.

## Letting the Other Person do the Majority of the Speaking

People like to talk; you would be well advised to let them do so. One of the simplest things you can do to endear yourself to other people is to be a good, genuinely interested listener. Being present is part of the equation but appearing engaged is even more important.

Over the years I've "mastered" the cadence of being spoken to well enough at this point simply by letting the words and facial expressions of the speaker naturally guide my own responses, reactions, and expressions. Even if the person were speaking another language, I am confident that I could nod knowingly, smile, and raise my eyebrows at the right times based on the speaker's tone and inflection. This "feedback" to the speaker is key in letting them know they're reaching you: no one wants to speak to someone with a flat, non-reactive affect.

## Try to see things from their point of view

There's no small amount of irony in the fact that one of the most important abilities in getting along well with other people is the ability to see things from their point of view, yet a key disability of autism is mindblindness. You might be an expert in convincing people to your *own* point of view, but to make new friends effectively, you might have to learn to see things from *their* points of view. As discussed in the chapter dedicated to the topic, many with mindblindness have a compromised ability to intuitively know what the other

> *"If there is any one secret of success, it lies in the ability to see things from the other person's angle as well as from your own."*

person is feeling about the subject at hand. With mindblindness, perhaps the best you might be able to do is to put yourself logically in their position--anticipating what will be most important to them. To the extent that you can anticipate their ideas and desires, you can ensure that whatever proposition or position you are advancing is at least consistent with them.

## A Daily Dose of Social

As someone who works at home, alone, on primarily creative undertakings, I do not spend a great deal of time these days working directly with other people. In the course of my day, I might awaken to my family and proceed to interact with a small handful of sales and customer service staff; perhaps I will meet a friend for lunch or coffee. But that is largely it, and my social needs and desires are more than met for another day.

It is not the case with my neurotypical wife. She knows hundreds of people from the local community and any number of seemingly important details about each of them, including their relationships to one another. Not only am I oblivious to the web of interpersonal complexity that swirls around everyone, but I also actively avoid it as though it were a quicksand that I risk becoming mired in if I get too close! Whereas I have noted elsewhere that I tend to remember people based almost solely on a functional, what-do-you-know-and-what-can-you-do basis, Nicole retains any number of other dimensions about a person: their likes, dislikes, aspirations, fears, and so much more.

Not only that, but Nicole also appears to enjoy learning all this social information about people in much the same way as I might learn about a complex new piece of shop equipment, like a mill or a lathe. Not only does she perceive a value or utility in learning everything there is to be learned about other people, but she also puts that information all to good productive use when some school or community event needs to be organized.

People like my wife seem to have an incredibly strong social sense and drive, and in fact, will actually crave such interaction if they are denied it too long. As I write this section, we are in the midst of the Coronavirus lockdowns. If these are trying times for individuals with autism, primarily due to their difficulty in accepting change, then they are also a very trying time for those neurotypical people who could accurately be described as "social butterflies."

Even before the lockdown, by the end of the day if my wife has not had a specific need to go out and interact with anyone, I am convinced she will formulate one and run to the store simply to get out of the house and see other people -- the more she knows whoever it is she sees, the better. I don't think my presence in the equation makes a difference either way -- if I come along visiting with other folks, I am at best a catalyst that doesn't participate in the reaction! Naturally, at some point, I questioned why I by myself was not enough to meet the bulk of Nicole's social needs, but I've long since made peace with the fact that being married to a social, neurotypical woman means sharing her, in a very real sense, with friends and relatives. Forty-five minutes of visiting and laughing with friends or relatives over a cup of coffee or a glass of wine provide a type of recharge that I alone cannot provide.

## A Reason for Being

The Japanese language has a special word for a life well invested: *ikigai*. Often translated more literally as "a reason for being," it is more than simply what is important to you; it is where you spend your time, where you invest your energy, where you expect to draw returns from, and where you will build your legacy. It is that which provides satisfaction, accomplishment, profit, and entertainment at the same time. More accurately, it is the union of what you love, where your passions lie, what you are good at doing, and what the world needs done.

Some may not have any idea what this thing is yet, while others may not even remember a time before they knew--for they have always known. In all cases, it is something naturally suited to the person's temperament; in fact, it is something they are good at doing. There is also a demand for the thing, and it is something that you could build a healthy profession out of providing. If something meets all these criteria *and* happens to be something that you love doing, you have found your Ikigai.

This might sound like it is too onerous of a filter: what are the odds that something can be so practical and yet also be beloved at the same time? Perhaps we would have a much better chance of success by starting with the things you love doing. If you have a special interest -- then you may already know at least one important part of the puzzle.

## Ikigai Diagram

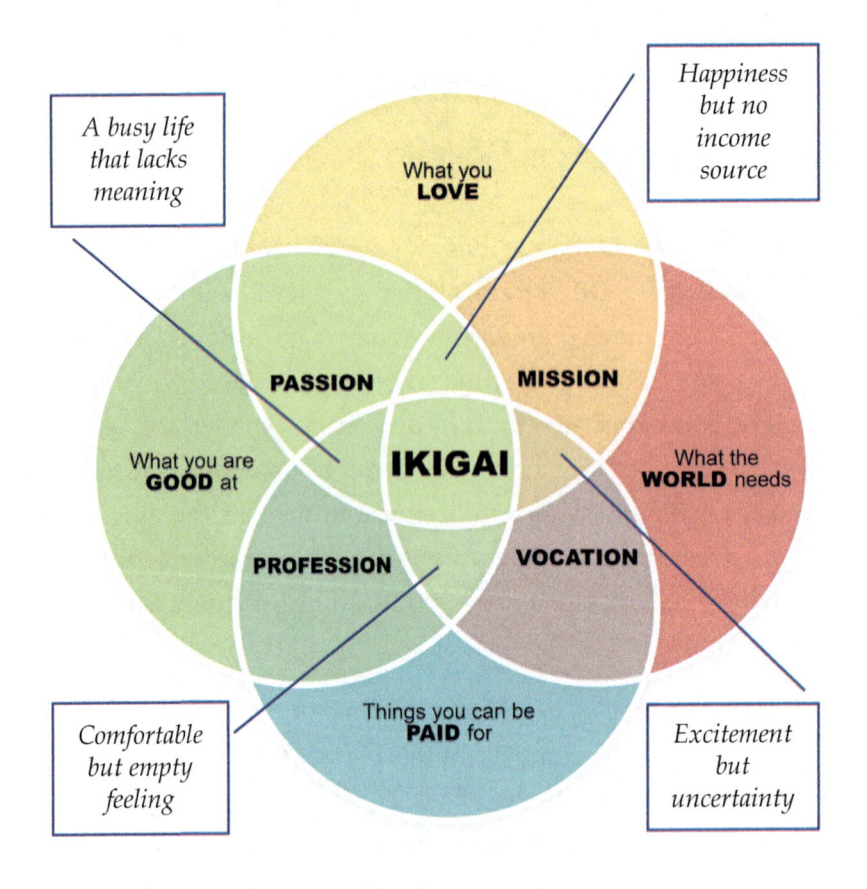

- *A busy life that lacks meaning*
- *Happiness but no income source*
- *Comfortable but empty feeling*
- *Excitement but uncertainty*

**What you LOVE** · **What you are GOOD at** · **What the WORLD needs** · **Things you can be PAID for**

**PASSION** · **MISSION** · **PROFESSION** · **VOCATION** · **IKIGAI**

If you begin with the things you love, the next natural foothold on the path to ikigai is to search amongst those things to find something that you seem to have a knack for. Your love of harp music is certainly a better candidate as a potential profession if you have some skill at playing the harp, or at least with music. But therein lies the trap: what if you were to pursue a profession that can never become a vocation for lack of paying customers? Unfortunately, it would be folly to do so, at least as a living; if there is no vocation in it, it is the stuff of hobbies unless you are independently wealthy!

As you can see from the diagram, something might approach being ikigai for you while being deficient in only one axis: if in the case of classical music only the ability to be paid for it is missing, you can certainly build a passion for it, and even make it your life's mission, and if you do it long enough you may be able to turn it into a profession. But if you cannot be paid for it, there is no vocation in it.

Helpful friends and relatives may seek to help find things that you are proficient at to see if a path can be found for you (not unlike my great innate aptitude for chicken farming and mortician work, perhaps). But what good would being the world's greatest air traffic controller be if, between flights, your mind is consumed with thoughts of classical music? Certainly, a profession is better than a career, which is better than a job, which is better than work, which is better than no work. Without love for what you are doing, however, whatever you do will always feel like hard work.

You have no doubt heard the old saw that reminds you to "Find a job you love, and you never have to work another day in your life." I'm here to remind you that it is true. All my life, from my first exposure, I had a love for technology, electricity, automation, and mechanization. When I then saw them all combined for the first time in the form of a computer, I loved it in a way that any kid might love a pinball machine or video game. The difference between them, however, is that it's very hard (though never impossible) to make a living at pinball or video games, whereas it would turn out to be reasonably easy to make a living programming computer (in fact, I even spent a few years professionally developing video games, but had no particularly unique passion for the gaming side).

## Opportunities that Fit

Imagine for a moment that your special interest is trains. Your ability to participate in the rail industry will vary with your ability, talents, and effort. Perhaps your task is as simple as to sweep up after hours at the local railway museum. Or perhaps you can secure a job with the railway company painting the numbers on tanker cars. You might be well suited to a job on the transportation side of things, working your way up to engineer or conductor over the years. Or perhaps you will attend college and receive the education necessary to begin design work on the massive turbodiesel V16 engines that power the enormous leviathans up front. Where you fit in will vary with your preferences, abilities, and the economic needs and opportunities that surround you.

If, after suitable research, nothing can be found, then perhaps it is time to consider that at least one or more of those factors must change and/or improve: your preferences, abilities, or opportunities. In my own case, I had to relocate to another nation to chase an opportunity, but you may also have local opportunities for which you simply need to hone or improve your abilities with practice, education, or experience.

## Sell Your Ability, Not Your Personality

Given the appropriate skills and experience, if you are sufficiently beautiful and affable, opportunities will quickly convert into lasting employment. For the rest of us, however, and particularly for those of us with autism, selling ourselves is not so easy. It is much more effective to sell our ability than our personality and presentation.

As professor Temple Grandin has noted, people with autism should carry a portfolio of their work and attempt to sell their ability, not themselves. Odds are that if you are attempting to secure a job in your field of special interest, you will have no shortage of previous effort to demonstrate, and you should be able to direct attention to what you do, and away from how you present, particularly if you think that presentation is hampering you relative to the other candidates. Carrying your portfolio digitally is fine, particularly if it's something you can send or forward.

"May I send you a sample of my work?" will garner much more attention, and have a much higher probability of success, than "Can I shoot you my resume?"

## A Fortuitous Videotape

After I had dropped out of high school, I wandered into a series of low-paying jobs that had nothing to do with my special interest in computer programming. One day, out of nowhere, a student that I had gone to high school with phoned me from the other side of the country, where he now lived. He wondered if I had kept up with programming (which I had) and would I be interested in a job programming video games?

"But of course!" howled my inner dialogue. Computer programming was all I was interested in. To secure the job, I offered to send them a videotape demonstrating that I knew how to code reasonably complicated scenarios such as video interrupts and sprite multiplexing. I stayed up long hours to complete the task promptly and sent a video off by FedEx. Two days later, I had a job offer and I was being asked how much salary I would need to accept the position--and we had never met.

Years later, to get my job at Microsoft, I was able to point to my own complex programs that I had developed and sold, and that made all the difference in the world in terms of getting an interview and securing an opportunity. There could be little doubting what I was able to do when I could demonstrate that I had already done it, and to what quality level.

Once I was a programmer at Microsoft, when I discovered another internal product (the Windows Shell) that I wished to work on, I just started tinkering with it on the side. When I later showed my work to the developers of that area, I was able to net an internal interview and eventually a job working on my favorite component. When I wished to start my own project and develop what would become known as the Windows Task Manager, rather than fancy proposals I simply wrote a working prototype in my spare time at home as a demonstration. That demonstration of ability was enough to secure a job working on my own pet project.

In each of these cases, the formal interview actually came last, really as a way of validating that I was not *too* out of the ordinary, but the technical decision on my abilities had already been made based on the merits of my past production and portfolio.

At each of these junctures, you will note, I did not merely apply for a position. I demonstrated that I could already do the job and that I could do it exceptionally well, by providing concrete portfolio examples. If your affect and presentation in an interview is an encumbrance when it comes to finding a job, you may very well find that demonstrating your ability is paramount over the in-person meeting. Employers might feel that they are taking a risk by hiring someone with autism, but concrete proof of your abilities will go a very long way towards assuaging any concerns they might have. It will also allow you to be upfront: "Yes, I may require some extra accommodation in the workplace, but I can produce what you need at a speed and level of quality second to none."

# Afterword

## The Ten-Second Autism Test

I've often joked that I have a ten-second autism test, and it goes something like this:

"Which is more important to society -- creativity or cooperation?"

As a gross generalization, I've found that neurotypical people generally lean towards cooperation, whereas those on the spectrum opt for creativity.

I've heard autism referred to as "the technology genes", and I think the notion has some merit. I would imagine that 100,000 years ago a teen tribe member became bored with the idle fireside gossip and wandered off to try to make the perfect arrowhead with a rock and some flint. With a flair for anticipating how it would fracture and a personality that demanded symmetry in all things, this tribal Tesla may have been one of the progenitors of the gene set that contributes to autism today. As Temple Grandin has speculated, without the genes responsible for autism we might all still be socializing around that campfire.

Does that mean that I believe creativity trumps cooperation? For several years, I actually did, until one day I realized there's something even more powerful than either.

And that, of course, is both in combination. A society sparked by the creativity of a few unique individuals and then fueled by the dedicated cooperation of the neurotypical. We don't all need to, as Steve Jobs put it, "Think Different." But it helps a great deal if at least a few do.

I'm not sure how other minds work since I've only experienced my own. But mine is very 3D and visual. For example, a computer program like the Windows Task Manager is really a complete little machine constructed in code. It has pumps and switches and even factories that make components. Just as a mechanical engineer might draw out the gears and cogs and cams needed for their conception, I first had a vision for how the machine would work and then defined it for the computer using a programming language. First, I made the parts, and then I assembled the parts into components, and components came together to form the machine, which is the program itself. Even 25 years later, I can still picture a good deal of the code in my mind.

I have a friend who played cornerback in the NFL, and one of his best "stadium moments" was a "pick 6" interception that he ran back for a touchdown in front of 80,000 screaming fans. When he told me about it, I noted that I would never have the opportunity to experience something like that (unless perhaps I learn to play the guitar soon)! But in the case of Task Manager, on average every month a billion people will use it, as they have for the last 25 years. Each day, I wake up knowing that a billion little copies of the machine that I dreamed up in my head are humming away on computers around the world.

Believe it not, for someone like myself, that's way bigger than a stadium of cheering fans. So, if you're running Windows, press CTRL-SHIFT-ESC and "Say Hello to my Little Friend!"

# Sources

### Photo of Steve Jobs, page 9

| | |
|---|---|
| Credit: | Matthew Riegler |
| Date: | 17 June 2007 |
| Source: | Wikimedia Commons |
| Modifications: | Subject masked and mirrored |

### Photo of David Plummer, page 85

| | |
|---|---|
| Credit: | Janet Plummer |
| Date: | 1969 |

### Central Coherence Illustration, page 138

| | |
|---|---|
| Credit: | Temple Grandin. Ph.D. |
| Source: | TED Talk |

*Used with Permission*

### Ikigai Illustration, page 266

| | |
|---|---|
| Credit: | Eric Plummer |
| Date: | 4 Oct 2021 |
| Modifications: | Text callouts added |

### Time Magazine Quote, page 82

(Time Magazine, 2018, April 26).

*Asperger's Syndrome, the Nazi Regime and the Dangerous Power of Labeling People.*

https://time.com/5255779/shhop-syndrome-nazi-germany-history/

## About the Author

According to Wikipedia, "David William Plummer is a Canadian-American programmer and entrepreneur. He created the Windows Task Manager, the Space Cadet Pinball game ports to Windows NT, Zip file support for Windows, HyperCache for the Amiga, and many other software products. He has been issued six patents in the software engineering space. He holds the world record score for the video game Tempest", and hosts Dave's Garage on YouTube.

David's diagnosis of Autism Spectrum Disorder came as a surprise -- at least to him -- and did not arrive until well into his adulthood. Although he always knew he was significantly different from most people, particularly in childhood, he had no idea that there were millions of people who were "similarly different."

Printed in Great Britain
by Amazon